THE CATHOLIC SHRINES OF EUROPE

THE CATHOLIC

BY THE RT. REV. *John K. Cartwright*

RECTOR, ST. MATTHEW'S CATHEDRAL, WASHINGTON, D.C.

WITH PHOTOGRAPHS BY *Alfred Wagg*

FOREWORD BY THE MOST REV. *Martin J. O'Connor*

TITULAR BISHOP OF THESPIAE

RECTOR OF THE NORTH AMERICAN COLLEGE, ROM

NEW YORK   TORONTO   LONDON

SHRINES *of* EUROPE

McGRAW-HILL BOOK COMPANY, INC.

THE CATHOLIC SHRINES OF EUROPE

Library of Congress Catalog Card Number: 54-11259

NIHIL OBSTAT: John Tracy Ellis, Censor Librorum

IMPRIMATUR: Patrick A. O'Boyle, Archbishop of Washington, D.C.:

May 17, 1954

PUBLISHED BY THE MC GRAW-HILL BOOK COMPANY, INC.

PRINTED IN THE UNITED STATES OF AMERICA

*To the Honorable and Mrs. Myron C. Taylor,
whose dedication to a deeper appreciation of
our civilization through our Christian heritage
has served as an inspiration to so many.*

ACKNOWLEDGMENT   The authors wish to thank the many persons at home and abroad who have assisted in the preparation of this book.

Mr. Wagg was assisted by a number of persons throughout Europe, ecclesiastical, diplomatic, and lay. Of these we wish particularly to thank the following: His Eminence Nicholas Cardinal Canali, President of the Pontifical Commission for Vatican City; His Eminence, Francis Cardinal Spellman, Archbishop of New York; The Most Reverend Martin J. O'Connor, Rector, North American College, Rome; The Most Reverend Gerald P. O'Hara, D.D., Apostolic Delegate to England; The Right Reverend Gustav J. Schultheiss of New York; The Right Reverend Joseph McGeough of the Vatican, Rome; The Right Reverend Thomas J. McMahon of New York; The Very Reverend David Cashman of London; The Reverend Francis U. O'Malley of London; The Reverend Gerald Hulme of Walsingham; The Reverend R. P. Ignacio Errandonea, S.J., of Loyola, Spain; the Daughters of Charity of St. Vincent de Paul, rue du Bac, Paris; Mother Mary Martin, Our Lady of Lourdes Hospital, Drogheda, Ireland.

Additionally we wish to thank: His Excellency, Mr. Myron C. Taylor, formerly personal representative of the President of the United States to his Holiness Pope Pius XII; Count Enrico Pietro Galeazzi, Architect of Sacred Apostolic Palaces and Special Delegate of the Pontifical Commission for Vatican City; The Honorable Paul Child, Public Affairs Officer, U.S.I.A., Marseilles, who contributed photographs of France and advised on photographic possibilities in France; The Duke of Luna, Director General of Tourism; The Honorable Gabriel Garcia-Loygorri, Secretary General and Staff, Spanish State Tourist Department, Madrid; The Honorable Mario Vannini Parenti, President, Tourist Bureau, Florence; The Honorable Russell Harris, U.S.I.A., Genoa; The Honorable Morrill Cody, American Information Service, Madrid; The Honorable John McKnight, Deputy Director, U.S.I.A., Rome; J. M. O'Laughlin, Press Section, British Foreign Office; Miss Phyllis Iliffe; Lt. Col. Hugh Day, Public Information, U.S.A.F.; Col. Paul Stanley Emrich, U.S.A.F.; Fogra Failte, National Tourist Publicity Organization for Ireland; French National Tourist Office in New York and Paris; Conte Sigmund Fago Golfarelli and staff of the Italian Tourist Bureau, Rome; D. A. Webb, Press Liaison Office and staff of the British Travel and Holiday Association, London; The Honorable James Moceri, Vice Consul, U.S.A., Florence; Lincoln White, Chief Press Information Officer, Department of State, Washington; Charles H. Campbell, American Director of British Information Services, Washington; Baron H. A. de Pfyffer d'Altishofen, Commandant of the Swiss Guard, Vatican City; John B. McCloskey, Delegate for France, National Catholic Welfare Conference; William Carney, formerly correspondent of *The New York Times* in Spain; John R. Cocker, banker, Washington, D.C.; Sn. Dn. Enrique Marsans, Director, Viajes Marsans (Travel Agency, Madrid); Sn. Dn. Jose Ignacio Domecq, Bodegas Domecq, Jerez, Spain.

On the picture production side, Pierre Gasmann of Pictorial Service, 17 rue de la Comete, Paris, was most helpful; also, Ralph Baum of Modernage Studios, New York. Other people helpful in production were: Sid Latham, who took the pictures of the Shrine of Fatima for Mr. Wagg; Sam Locker of Royaltone, Inc., New York; the Hamilton Wright Organization, Inc., Rockefeller Plaza, New York; Frank Rizzatti of Burleigh Brooks Co. (American Representative of Rolleiflex), New York; Capt. John F. Kerwin of the Cosmopolitan Shipping Co., New York; and Pan American World Airways. The following are also to be thanked for their contribution of photographs to the book: Swiss National Tourist Office; Austrian Information Service, New York (Dr. Eugen Buresch, Director); German Tourist Information Office; Netherlands Information Service; National Tourist Office, Luxembourg; Sabena Belgian World Airlines; Official Belgian Tourist Bureau.

In addition to the above, Monsignor Cartwright wishes particularly to thank the following who have assisted in the preparation of the text: The Reverend John Tracy Ellis of Washington, D.C., and Miss Alma Savage of New York.

FOREWORD

SPEAKING AS ONE WHO HAS LIVED in Europe for many years may I
say that it gives me great satisfaction to contribute a foreword to
the volume *The Catholic Shrines of Europe,* which is now presented
to the public by The Rt. Rev. John K. Cartwright of Washington,
D.C., and by Mr. Alfred Wagg, whose photography is so well
known in the United States.

When Mr. Wagg first came to me in Rome he carried a letter
from His Excellency, Mr. Myron C. Taylor, formerly the personal
representative of the President of the United States to His Holiness
Pope Pius XII. Mr. Taylor's encouragement of this artist led to my
own personal interest and assistance in the project and likewise to
the hope that his work would be most successful.

However, this was only the beginning, for in my conversation
with Mr. Wagg I developed an enthusiastic interest in his plan to
bring home to people, especially in the United States, the beauty
and the significance of the Catholic Shrines of Europe. I saw in this
effort an attempt to popularize the content of the European tradition and treasure house of culture and a happy chance of proving
once again how the building of our great Western civilization,
wherein lie our American roots, was a process involving centuries
and genius and the Catholic Church.

Since 1948 more than 150,000 American citizens have visited
the North American College in Rome. As a rule, their purpose is to
present an application to be received by His Holiness. Nearly one-
third of these visitors are either Protestants or Jews. In the past few
years I have talked with many of those who have come to the
College and out of all this vast multitude it has been the rare exception who has not been fascinated by our Christian heritage of art
and architecture as it covers the face of Europe.

So we say that this is a most interesting travel experience for
those who are anxious to renew memories of their trips to Europe.

Indeed we hope that many will prepare for their European journeys by reading it carefully. One could plan a series of interesting visits to various places from the materials supplied and have a treasure house there of valuable memories.

One day a lady who was really much-traveled, in answer to my question as to how she liked Rome, told me that "all big cities were the same"! Of course, such a radical discount of the historical and religious values of the Eternal City is confined to the opinion of pitifully few people, for the vast majority are enthralled by the majesty, beauty, and dignity of all that is best in the cultural core of our Western civilization.

The authors of this book bring to their task more than adequate preparation. The text which accompanies the pictures is the work of a distinguished Washington priest, the Rt. Rev. John K. Cartwright, who is now the pastor of the beautiful Cathedral of St. Matthew in Washington, D.C. Monsignor Cartwright has a national reputation as a lecturer and writer and is the Founder and Director of the Critics' Forum in Washington. A graduate of the North American College in Rome, he was also Professor of Church History at the Sulpician Seminary at the Catholic University of America and Assistant Professor of Pastoral Theology as well.

Alfred Wagg's unique career of author, lecturer, photographer, world traveler, and foreign correspondent, has taken him around the world time and time again and has brought him into such widely different places as Hyderabad, the heart of the Arabian desert, and the White House. His technical preparation and unwavering interest in his subject, whether it is the Ardagh Chalice or the Cathedral of Burgos, the Basilica at Paray-le-Monial or Bernini's canopy in St. Peter's, will lead you to some of the most interesting and fascinating places in Europe. His appreciation of people will make you long remember the choir boys at Auray, the Swiss Guards, a medical missionary at Drogheda. He has an unusual and an exquisite touch in selecting and recording masterpieces of God as well as those of men.

May this volume therefore find its way into the homes of the traveled as well as into the hands of those who will confine their wanderings to the space between its covers.

Martin J. O'Connor

CONTENTS

PATHWAYS OF CHRISTIANITY *page 1*

Mamertine Prison, Rome; St. Lazarus; St. Mary Magdalen; St. Martha; les Saintes Maries de la Mer, Provence; Church of St. Victor, Marseilles; Church of Vera Cruz, Segovia, Spain; Santiago de Compostela, Spain; Puente del Arzobispo, Spain; Walsingham, England; the Rock of Cashel, Ireland.

ROME AND THE VATICAN *page 17*

St. Peter's; Tomb of St. Peter; chapel of the Blessed Sacrament; tombs of the popes; the Vatican; Vatican guards; mosaic factory; Vatican gardens and fountains; papal palace at Avignon, France; St. John Lateran; St. Mary Major; St. Paul Without the Walls.

ITALY *page 49*

San Miniato, Florence; Villa Schifanoia, Florence; shrines of Our Lady; Santa Maria de la Guardia, Genoa; Our Lady of Pompeii; Sanctuary of Loreto; Assisi; tomb of St. Francis; relics of St. Francis; Basilica of St. Francis of Assisi; paintings by Giotto; the Franciscan monastery; Church of St. Clare; St. Anthony of Padua; shrine of the Holy Shroud, Turin; Siena; the Certosa at Pavia; Santa Maria della Salute, Venice.

FRANCE *page 75*

Notre Dame; St. Germain des Prés, Paris; St. Séverin, Paris; Chartres; Bourges; Laon; Toùrs; Poitiers; Abbaye aux Hommes, Caen; St. Bernard; Cistercian monasteries; Church of the Madeleine, Vézelay; Strasbourg; Dijon; Cathedral of St. Cecilia, Albi; les Saintes Maries de la Mer; Nôtre Dame de la Garde, Marseilles; LePuy; Joan of Arc; Orcival; Conques; the Sisters of Charity; St. Catherine Labouré; St. Vincent de Paul; St. Theresa of Lisieux; Mont St. Michel; Brittany; Quimper; Lourdes.

SPAIN *page 113*

The Alcázar, Segovia; the Escorial; Toledo; Our Lady of Covadonga; St. James the Apostle; Santiago de Compostela; Our Lady of the Pillar, Saragossa; Salamanca; Valladolid; St. Theresa of Avila; Burgos; San Domingo de Silos; the cathedral at Segovia; San Isidoro, León; "the Catholic Kings"; Granada; Seville; the Giralda; tomb of Columbus; monastery of La Rabida; Palos de la Frontera; Guadalupe; Montserrat; Loyola; St. Ignatius.

PORTUGAL *page 145*

Our Lady of Fatima.

GERMANY   *page 151*

  *Kalkar; Kiedrich; St. Boniface; Fulda; Hildesheim; Maria-Laach; Cathedral of
  Cologne; Bad Oberdorf; Marburg; Creglingen; Nuremberg; Cathedral of Aachen;
  Worms; Mainz; Limburg; Altotting; Vierzehnheiligen; Fürstenfeldbrück; Zweifal-
  ten; Weiskirche; Bierbach; Ettal; Oberammergau.*

AUSTRIA AND SWITZERLAND   *page 163*

  *Heiligenkreuz (Holy Cross Monastery); Melk; Lilienfeld; Gurk; Gottweig; Klos-
  terneuberg; Altenburg; Mondsee; St. Wolfgang; Maria Saal; Mauer. St. Gall,
  Switzerland; Einsiedeln; Madonna del Sasso at Locarno.*

THE LOW COUNTRIES   *page 171*

  *St. Augustine in Amsterdam; St. Servatus in Maastricht; Valkhof Chapel in
  Nijmegen; St. John in s'Hertogenbosh. Mariental, Luxembourg; St. Maurice and
  St. Maur, Clervaux; Cathedral of Notre Dame, Luxembourg City; Echternach;
  St. Willibrord. Aarschatt, Belgium; Hal; Tongres; St. Hubert; Pommeroeil;
  Braine-le-Comte; Furnes; Ostende; St. Michael and St. Gudule, Brussels; Notre
  Dame at Antwerp; St. Rombaut, Malines; belfry and St. Baron, Ghent; Notre
  Dame at Tournai; Notre Dame and Chapel of the Precious Blood, Bruges; Orval.*

IRELAND   *page 181*

  *St. Patrick; Gallerus Oratory; the Hill of Slane; St. Patrick's Church, Belfast;
  Downpatrick Cathedral; the legendary grave of St. Patrick; Lough Derg; St.
  Kevin's Church, Glendaloch; St. Brigid's Wall; Clonmacnois; the Cross of Cong;
  the Ardagh Chalice; St. Patrick's Bell; the Book of Dimma; the Book of Kells;
  the Rock of Cashel; Sligo Abbey; Muckross Abbey; Hoare Abbey; Mt. Melleray
  Church; Drogheda; Oliver Plunket; Maynooth College; Our Lady of Dublin; the
  Church of Christ the King, Cork; Killarney.*

ENGLAND   *page 203*

  *St. Etheldreda's, London; Glastonbury Abbey; Lanercost Priory; Our Lady of
  Walsingham; the Silver Slipper Chapel, Walsingham; Westminster Cathedral.*

COLOR PLATES

	facing page
Swiss Guards and Sisters of Charity before St. Peter's, Rome	20
Statue of St. Peter, St. Peter's, Rome	21
Swiss Guards, Vatican City	36
Sisters of Atonement, spire of St. Clare, Assisi	37
Franciscan Brother near Assisi	116
Cathedral at Salamanca, Spain; Tomb of St. James, Compostela	117
Pilgrimage at Clonmacnois, Ireland	132
Grey Abbey, Ireland	133

MAP OF THE SHRINES   *pages 2 and 3*

THE CATHOLIC SHRINES OF EUROPE

PATHWAYS OF CHRISTIANITY

CHRISTIANITY, AND SPECIFICALLY CATHOLIC Christianity of which these pages treat, came into the world at a given moment of history and in a given place in the lands of the eastern Mediterranean. It now exists in every quarter of the earth. The story of its spread is a fascinating part of history.

Christianity is not merely an idea or, as the saying now goes, an "ideology." It is not merely an inspiration, an enthusiasm, or a spiritual impulse. It is all these but it is more. It is a society, a church embodying and interpreting an idea. It is a gathering of people giving outlet and expression to the spiritual impulse.

This social form is not the casual consequence of the promulgation of the idea. It is the will and the purpose of the Founder. Christ was not content with teaching His idea and leaving it to find its way in the world. He established the Church to take care of the idea.

Old Roman bridge at Puente del Arzobispo, Spain.

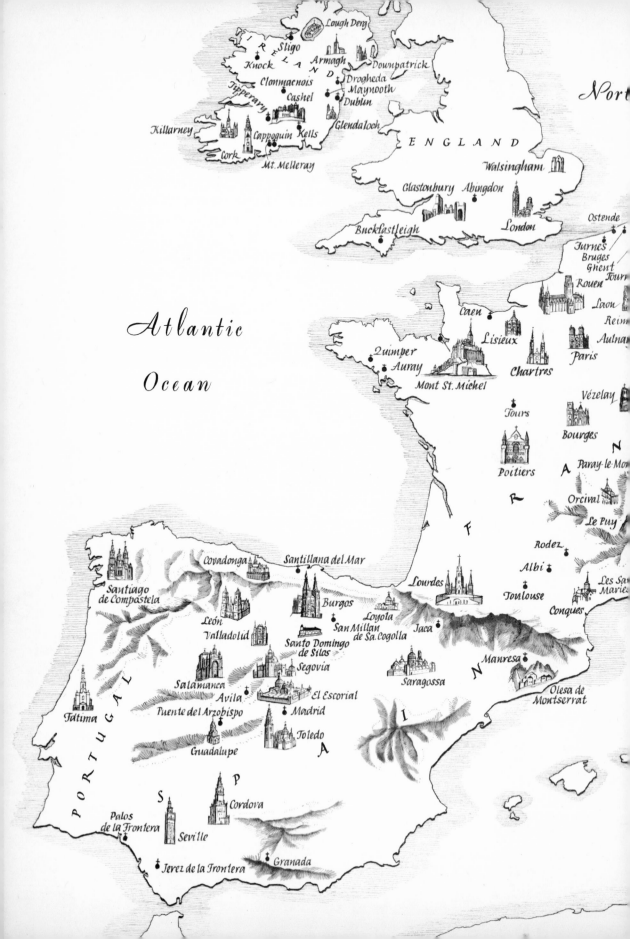

IRELAND

Lough Derg
Sligo
Knock
Armagh
Downpatrick
Clonmacnois
Drogheda
Cashel
Maynooth
Tipperary
Dublin
Killarney
Cappoquin Kells
Glendaloch
Cork
Mt. Melleray

ENGLAND

Walsingham
Glastonbury Abingdon
London
Buckfastleigh

Nort

Ostende

Furnes
Bruges
Ghent
Tour
Rouen
Caen
Laon
Reim
Lisieux
Aulna
Chartres
Paris
Quimper
Auray
Mont St. Michel

Atlantic

Ocean

Vézelay
Tours
Bourges
Poitiers
Paray-le-Mon

A

F

R

N

Orcival
Le Puy
Rodez
Albi
Les Sa
Maries
Conques

Covadonga
Santillana del Mar
Santiago
de Compostela
Lourdes
Burgos
Toulouse
León
Loyola
Jaca
Valladolid
San Millán
de Sa. Cogolla
Santo Domingo
de Silos
Manresa
Segovia
Salamanca
Saragossa
Olesa de
Montserrat
Avila
El Escorial
Fátima
Puente del Arzobispo
Madrid
Toledo
A
Guadalupe
I

PORTUGAL

S
P
Cordova
Palos
de la Frontera
Seville
Jerez de la Frontera
Granada

Since His time on earth the Church has been with humanity, taking care of His idea and carrying out the mission to make "all nations" His disciples. In its universality the mission has not yet been completed. But in the universal tendency and purpose there has been no truce through sixty generations of man's history.

The effort has made its imprint chiefly upon souls. But souls are in bodies and move in space and make use of material elements for their purposes. An institution, therefore, which has impressed so many souls and which has had as its purpose to unite them cannot fail to have left many traces upon the surface of the earth.

So it is possible to see the Church in the places and buildings wherein its constituency of souls has gathered. Even one who stands outside, looking with some sympathy and desire to understand so great a historical phenomenon, can at least appreciate the corporate dimensions of the Church and can measure the increase and extent of its influence by its buildings and what happens in them. Today a great many persons travel over large surfaces of the earth and are in a position to measure the "catholicity" of Catholicism by the omnipresence of its activities. To have seen the majesty of the Easter service in St. Peter's and the humble sweetness of May devotions in a mission of Guam or Nigeria is to have learned a great deal about something very important to mankind. This sort of realization is more easily come by today than in the past.

The actual presence and contemporary effectiveness of the Church is self-evident. But those with historical feeling can also make their own measurements. Just as we gauge the present-day Church by the places which it actually occupies, so we can estimate the growth or recession of its life through the ages by the shrines and temples in which the generations have worshiped.

This volume deals only with the shrines of Europe, and

of necessity, with a selection of those. This is not a concession to the notion that Catholicism is a purely European thing in the way that, years ago, Hilaire Belloc gave currency to the phrase: "The Faith is Europe and Europe is the Faith." Europe does not contain enough to represent the universal Church, but it has been, historically, the place of the longest and most dominant activity of the Church. It is the site of the earliest and most successful spread of Christian doctrines and institutions. The modern peoples of Western Europe date back to a blending of heterogeneous elements of race and language in a period of from ten to sixteen centuries ago. Over that blending Christianity presided. In the progress of the new peoples out of the turmoil of the Dark Ages, their chief institution, not only religious but cultural, was the Church. In their efforts to break out into new forms of intellectual and artistic life, she was their teacher. Above all, when they found the way to create new artistic forms in the period from the eleventh to the sixteenth century, it was in ecclesiastical channels that artists worked. Therefore, pictorially speaking, it is Europe which of necessity is the richest museum of those monuments of beauty and of faith.

The countries considered in this chapter on the pathways of Christianity are those which developed their religion from the original missionary impulses in the days of the Empire, before the "wandering of the peoples" gave geographical settings for the modern nations of Europe. This religious development took place between the reigns of Peter and Gregory the Great (590–604), coinciding with the age of the Church Fathers. In point of dogmatic teaching it is the time when the first six general councils laid down the doctrines which came to differentiate the orthodox Catholic from the sectarian or heterodox. Above all, it was the time when the original outburst of enthusiasm for the faith maintained its original pulsation. In this time those peoples became Catholic who occupied the lands now known as Italy, France, Spain,

Mamertine Prison, Rome, showing the pillar to which, according to legend, Peter and Paul were chained, and the hole through which they drew water.

Portugal, Ireland, and England, along with those parts of Germany west of the Rhine. In other words, the parts of western Europe which had been Roman now became Catholic. With Ireland added, the set was given to the great sequence of centuries during which, down to and including our own time, these countries came to be and remained the older children of the Church.

In this chapter the places which illustrate this primary spread of the faith are singled out. The pictures are not of buildings contemporary with this period, from which so little of architectural or artistic legacy has come down to us in original form, but they have been selected because they represent the places taken over by the faith and because, so to speak, they cover the territory.

The Mamertine is an ancient prison dating from the days of the Roman Republic. In it, by a barbarity which was then customary and which Christianity had abolished (only to find it coming into fashion again in some parts of the world), several famous enemies of Rome were kept before their execution. Among them were Jugurtha, the Numidian king, and Vercingetorix, the chieftain who maintained the last effective struggle of the Gauls against the Roman conquest under Caesar. According to a late legend, Peter also was imprisoned here. The story is that here Peter converted and baptized his jailers, Processus and Martinian, who afterward became martyrs, following his example. They were buried outside the walls in a catacomb that took its name from them, and later their relics were brought back to rest near those of Peter in his basilica.

Whether or not the details are true, the story is most illustrative. Peter was a prisoner in Rome and was put to death for the faith. And Peter did begin there the marvellous reversion of fortune which was to bring the greatest enemy of the faith to its knees. Some who knew Peter in prison might well have felt that all was against him—power, prestige, tradition, the common opinion of society. But to deeper minds—his jailers', perhaps—he represented a force that was new, and stronger than all the rest. Rome, which had built so much that was magnificent, had also made the Mamertine. But Rome, pagan Rome, was a force that was spent. And Peter was a force that was growing. In Peter's own time, hundreds of people like Processus and Martinian made that estimate against the odds that the rest of the world gave them. As it turned out, "he who was on the side of Peter was on the winning side."

In 1870 at the Vatican Council, the Papacy achieved

one of its greatest historical moments in the definition of In-
fallibility. At that moment the Council was assembled in the
right transept of the basilica. The throne of Pope Pius IX
was erected at the altar of SS. Processus and Martinian. Here
was a very meaningful illustration of the enduring life of that
impulse of faith and grace which came to Rome with the mission of its greatest prisoner and apostle.

After Italy itself one of the earliest parts of southern
Europe to be occupied by the conquering faith was the
Mediterranean coast of France. The authentic, documented
history of the Church in France begins in the second century
with the martyrdoms at Vienne and Lyons, a hundred miles
or so deep in the Rhone Valley. The religion of Christ took
hold—it could hardly be otherwise—in the well-populated
and long-settled towns of the Roman colonization, "the Province" par excellence, from which Provence takes its name.
Here was the city of Marseilles, a trading point for many
centuries and, in the time of the apostles, perhaps the most
important city of the Empire west of Rome.

The exact account of how the early Christians settled
here is wanting. But the glowing and romantic imagination of
the Middle Ages worked at the construction of many beautiful
stories. The most important of these was that of the saints of
Bethany, who were thought to be the apostles of this part of
Christendom.

St. Lazarus, whom our Lord raised from the dead; his
sisters, Mary Magdalen and Martha; the two other Marys (she
of Cleophas and Salome, who were concerned with our Lord's
burial and resurrection); St. Maximin and others who came
from Palestine or Ephesus—all ended their lives here in this
region of Provence. St. Lazarus would have been the first
bishop of Marseilles. St. Martha came to embody the symbol
of the faith overcoming the enemies of civilization, represented by a dragon called in French the *Tarasque*. She was
reported to have been buried at Tarascon where her tomb was

venerated. St. Mary Magdalen, bringing with her the remainder of the balsam with which our Lord had been anointed, dedicated herself to a life of isolation and prayer in a spot now called, after the holy relic which she carried, La Sainte Baume. She was first buried nearby in the church dedicated to St. Maximin; afterward her relics were taken to Vézelay in Burgundy and became the center of a most celebrated place of pilgrimage.

Several of the pictures in this chapter and in the one on France have to do with this legend of Bethany. The crypt of the Church of St. Victor in Marseilles has carvings dating back to the fifth century. One of these, reproduced here, is thought to be intended for a portrait of St. Lazarus. It was done, of course, at a time when the troubles of the old Mediterranean cities had brought culture and the arts, particularly the plastic arts, to a very low point of decline. But with such means as they had at their disposal, the monks of the time, who were maintaining the light of faith and letters in this, one of the pre-universities of the Dark Ages, maintained also the tradition of sculpture, transmitting the faint spark of beauty to be warmed into fairer life at the coming of a more fortunate day.

Les Saintes Maries de la Mer (The Holy Marys of the Sea) is built on what is supposed to have been their landing place on their arrival from Palestine. When Lazarus, Martha and Mary Magdalen went farther inland, Mary of Cleophas and Mary Salome stayed with their servant Sarah on the shore and lived out their years there. A church was built to enshrine their remains and, after long centuries, it was destroyed by the Saracens in the Dark Ages. With the persistence of reverential memories, the people of the twelfth century built another church, and with the prudence of their time, made it a fort as well. The parapets still bespeak their time, as does the well within the church for the provision of the place when besieged.

The paradox of a shrine with battlements reminds us of a

time when, as in our own day, men had to fight to preserve
the things they held dearest. Originally an island, the site has
been joined to the land for many ages now, and on the south
the sea has retreated, as it does constantly before the deposits
of earth brought down between the two arms of the Rhone
Delta. This delta, the Camargue, is a land of loneliness. Long
subject to fever and inhospitable to large populations, it has
become a pasture for herds of almost wild cattle, a spread of
saltflats, and a kind of natural preserve for wild flowers and
such trees as frequent isolation, like umbrella pines, and for
birds that are always happier in places that men call lonely.
This is a land of loneliness, but not of desolation, for the
ancient church speaking of "melancholy far-off things and
battles long ago" speaks also of the spiritual—which is the
opposite of desolation. It is a place of pilgrimage in May and
October, and among those who come there for the festivities
are the Gypsies, one of the nomad peoples of the world, who
have taken this place to their hearts for many generations.

*Front façade of Les Saintes Maries de la
Mer, Provence.*

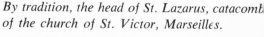

*By tradition, the head of St. Lazarus, catacomb
of the church of St. Victor, Marseilles.*

Wood carving of St. Mary Magdalen, Carthusian monastery, Marseilles.

Church of Vera Cruz at Segovia, Spain, consecrated in 1208.

Stone pillar, which is kissed by pilgrims to Santiago de Compostela, Spain.

Spain, like France, was slow in keeping records of its earliest Christian days. Yet we know that Paul considered going there, for he himself said so, and St. Clement in the first century and St. John Chrysostom in the fourth suggest that he went. This would seem to argue that even in Paul's time communities of Christians were living there.

There are venerable traditions to the effect that Christianity in Spain owed its beginning to Paul. There is also a very ancient report that the country was visited by James the Greater, the brother of John. The Church of Spain may thus be of doubly apostolic origin. The great shrine of Compostela, located on the northwest coast, was symbolic of the universality of the Church in the eyes of Roman citizens, Christian or pagan. To them the ocean was as outer space, and Spain, bordering on the ocean, was the end of the earth. The gospel had thus been carried to a point beyond which it had no farther to go. The column of Compostela may stand as a milepost at the western end of early Christianity's pathways.

The story of the progress of Christianity in the "ancient" period of Church history comprises also England and Ireland. But before leaving the Continent, we should remember that a characteristic of the time when "antiquity" was giving way to the Middle Ages is the fact that the faith, having reached its oceanic borders, turned back to make new pathways in Northern and Central Europe. The countries where the church had been so rapidly established began to send out impulses that resulted in the conversion of new peoples and regions. The great missionary figures are Saints Columbanus and Gall from Ireland, and Willibrord and Boniface from England. With their companions and successors and with contemporary movements from Italy and France, they introduced the faith to the areas of Low Countries, the Rhineland, the Vosges, the Jura, and along the east-west axis of the Alps in Switzerland, Bavaria, and Austria.

The appearance of Christianity in England is in line with its general development in all the settled Roman provinces. The apostolic process here, as in other lands, followed the Roman roads. St. Patrick, who afterward became a high ecclesiastic, was the son of a Roman colonial in Britain. When St. Patrick made his apprenticeship to the priesthood in France of the fifth century he could talk to his bishop, St. Germanus, of his own native country as part of Christendom.

But Ireland was out of the pale of the Roman Empire and did not enter in any effective literary way into the records which paint for us the picture of those early times. It is sure that in the fifth century Christians did live there: a mysterious figure named Palladius seemed to be the head of the Church in Ireland in Pre-Patrician times. But contacts with the mainland of Europe were few and far between, and the most definite knowledge we have of contacts between Britain and Ireland is the fact of pirate raids, such as the one which later carried the young Patrick into slavery there. The rest is legend: one we know is the basis of the greatest of Wagner's music-dramas, *Tristan and Isolde.*

The Rock of Cashel stands, as well as anything in Ire-

Remaining arch at Walsingham, England, demolished in 1538.

The Rock of Cashel, Tipperary, Ireland, visited by St. Patrick in 450 A.D.

land does, as the symbol of the political, ecclesiastic, and cultural life of the early Irish. It is given here as marking another terminal point of the period during which Christianity was striking out on its earliest pathways.

Ireland became part of the Western civilization by becoming Christian. The story of England was far more complicated. But here we have introduced the pathetic ruins of Walsingham to remind us of the essential part played by England in the early spread of the faith and in the establishment of Christendom.

Such are the outlines of the map; now for the details.

ROME AND
THE VATICAN

NOTHING STARTLES THE VISITOR TO ROME more than the aspect she wears of a modern city. This appearance was caused by her enormous growth during the period of Fascism and especially during and after World War II. Building by building, street after street, she has advanced on all sides into the neighboring Campagna. But perhaps the most forceful evidence of modernity is the traffic. In this respect Rome rivals Paris itself. There is a type of tourist, tired of sightseeing "history and art," who, when he sees the long line of cars waiting for the green light and has to watch out for the little Italian motorcycles called Vespe (Wasps) which make street-crossing an adventure, is likely to be pleased and comforted that progress is still going on, and surprised that there is no place which appears more progressive than this most venerable of cities. Then, aside from "the audience," to which he does give a special place in his schedule and afterward (God bless him) in his heart,

Dome of St. Peter's from the Pope's private garden.

he may leave Rome none the wiser for most of the marvelous things she has to teach him.

If his approach is that of the pilgrim rather than of the tourist, however, our traveler will inevitably find more of the real character of Rome, for Rome has been at work continuously for twenty-six centuries. She is not like Persepolis or Nineveh or Memphis, whose stones indicate that they flourished ages ago and gave what they had to give and then ceased; she is not like Paris or London, which are still living centers of civilization but whose lifetime as great centers has been much shorter than hers. Rome began to give the world something immensely important from the first. It was because she had something indispensable that she was able to build what we call her Empire. It was because of her place of eminence that the apostles Peter and Paul made her the capital of Christ's Church. Afterward the things that the pagan empire could no longer administer passed over to the custody of the Church and through her came down to us. And today when the din of the up-to-date is deafening in her streets, she is still the representative and heart of the universality of the faith which was planted by the apostles and watered by the blood of the victims of the Coliseum and the Mamertine.

Since Rome has meant so much and for so many centuries, and since places that mean much express their meaning in monuments, it follows that here the wealth of such expression is incomparable, more than incomparable, for it is the expression of a past which still lives.

The central interest of Rome is of course at the Vatican. It was once said that this is the area which contains the greatest church, the greatest palace, and the greatest tomb in the world. The last third of the statement would not be true, but the rest stands good as our pictures will show.

The Vatican is a hill, so called from pagan times. It is not, however, one of the "seven hills" of Rome, all of which are across the Tiber in what was the real city of ancient times and in what is the most extensive part of the modern city. Neither is it a high hill, but rather an elevation above the river level just sufficient to make a terrace for the majestic church and dome of St. Peter's and for the inimitable colonnade of Bernini which opens its arms to greet you.

Since the removal of two or three blocks of unimpressive buildings, the vista of St. Peter's is complete from the riverbank about half a mile distant and even from across the Tiber. Thus it is possible to approach the Vatican by a long walk during which the whole structure is visible before you.

One of the things to be seen on a leisurely approach is the beauty of St. Peter's color. The body of the church itself is made of travertine, one of the sturdiest of building stones but especially precious here because it is the finest of all stones for keeping its characteristic warm buff quality in spite of the dust of centuries. Above the body of the church is the glorious dome whose leaden coating has acquired a patina of blue that makes it even more beautiful than it would be by reason of its elegant outline.

Not everyone seems to know the fine story that is told of Michelangelo. The building had been carried to completion in large part by Sangallo the Younger. After his death the dome was still to be erected. So Pope Paul III called Michelangelo, who had years before painted the Sistine Chapel and carved the *Pietà,* to exercise the third of his great arts in raising "the Pantheon above St. Peter's." It is said that when Michelangelo left Florence he looked back from the hill of San Miniato and gazed at the dome which Brunelleschi had raised over Santa Maria del Fiore more than a century before. His concept of St. Peter's was not yet developed, apparently, for he is said to have remarked, as if talking to the Florence dome about the Roman one: "Like you I will not. Better than you I cannot."

Whether Michelangelo would have made it better we cannot know, for it was not completed until thirty years after his death. As it stands, it owes perhaps as much to Giacomo della Porta as it does to him. But when it was finished it transcended its great forerunner in Florence and became what it remains—the greatest of all domes over the greatest of all the Catholic shrines of Europe, and a symbol of the majesty of Rome's spiritual and greatest empire.

The site of St. Peter's was determined by the fact that his death had taken place here on the Vatican in Nero's circus and that his body was buried here a short time afterward. One of his near successors built some kind of a shrine here even before the persecutions were over. Less than a century after Peter's death there is historic evidence that even then it was a place of pilgrimage. Later, at a time of acute disturbance, the relics seem to have been temporarily removed to the catacombs. But when, after the dawn of the Church's peace, it became possible to raise places of worship and to maintain an order and splendor of public devotion, one of the first actions of that period of generous dreams was to build a noble church over Peter's resting place. This church, added to and embellished by the devotion of many generations, had a history of thirteen centuries. From the days of Constantine to those of Columbus it was the great pilgrimage center of Europe and of Latin Christendom. The list of names of the great ones of the earth who came here is a thrilling one, partly because each one of them stood for millions of others whose names only God knoweth: Theodosius and Valentinian, emperors; Belisarius, the Byzantine general and Totila of the Goths; five or six of the Saxon kings, and Alfred the Great himself, who came as a little prince with his father; the fabulous Charlemagne who was crowned here by Leo III.

But the venerable church which they saw has long passed away except for the fragments in the crypt and for two fragments in the great portico. The principal gates of the modern basilica are of bronze, cast in Florence in the last days of the old church and carried over to the new. Over them in the

Swiss Guards and Sisters of Charity before main façade of St. Peter's.

Statue of St. Peter in the nave of St. Peter's.

ceiling of the portico is another relic of the old church, Giotto's mosaic of Peter walking on the sea. The picture of this mosaic is unusual in that it was taken from a viewpoint just opposite on a dangerously narrow cornice of the portico. The mosaic is one of the very special treasures of St. Peter's, both because it came from the old church and because of its authorship. Giotto, the father of Italian painting, did very little of his work in Rome. But he was commissioned for this at the time of the first great jubilee of the year 1300. The subject of the picture, the ship riding the stormy waves and Peter saved from them, represents appropriately the storms through which the Church has survived the ages. It is said that Cardinal Baronius never passed into the church without making reverence to this picture. As a historian he was well equipped to understand its symbolism.

At the left end of the portico is a statue of the Emperor Charlemagne opposite the companion equestrian statue of the Emperor Constantine. They both belong here. They were human beings and had their faults. But they had great dreams for the world and, unlike some dreamers of today, they found place in their dreams of world betterment for Christ's Church and for the primacy of the spiritual. Later ages may bring new trophies to St. Peter's, but these two will always belong there.

You enter the door and the basilica is before you in all its magnificence.

The most arresting feature of the great expanse is the Canopy of St. Peter's Tomb directly under the dome. This canopy of bronze supported by twisted columns of the same material was designed by Bernini in 1633. Bernini was one of the chief masters, perhaps the chief, of the architectural style called Baroque. He designed the celebrated colonnade in the plaza before St. Peter's; he made also the monumental bronze chair in the apse of the church which contains the remains of Peter's pontifical throne. But the canopy here is probably his chief masterpiece, the one which dominates the memory most clearly when other features are forgotten.

There was a time when it was universally fashionable to make little of this Baroque style with its bold and startling departure from architectural repose. But today most writers on art seem to have come around to quite a different point of view. Meanwhile Bernini's colonnade and canopy have stood through the years, admirable when they were not admired and admirable now that they are admired. A great many people have always admired them, both when it was not correct to admire them and now that it is proper again. This seems to me to be symbolic of a great many things about the Church. Even when the "authorities" are agreed against her, a great many simple people are completely ignorant of what the authorities think. They just do their own thinking and love the Church in their own obstinate way. Then a fashion changes and the simple people come into good company again. And very often they know no more about the approval of the good company

(Opposite) St. Peter walking on the water, a mosaic by Giotto over the main entrance to the portico of St. Peter's. Hidden in a recess, this art treasure is likely to be overlooked by the visitor.

Portico of St. Peter's showing statue of Charlemagne.

when they have it than they knew about the disapproval when they had that.

The shrine itself has eighty-six lamps of gold which burn continually about the tomb of the fisherman of Galilee. Down in the chapel we shall see the kneeling statue of Pius VI who was pope when our Constitution was written. The statue by Canova is one of the finest in the church, seeming to portray one whose breathing has been arrested while his soul is absorbed in prayer. At the altar of the chapel is the relief of Peter healing the cripple. In the crypt (the ancient St. Peter's) lies an antique marble coffin in which are interred the remains of a great Roman civil dignitary, the Prefect of the City, Junius Bassus who died fifteen hundred years ago. This is mentioned as a sample of what the ancient St. Peter's has to show, for the

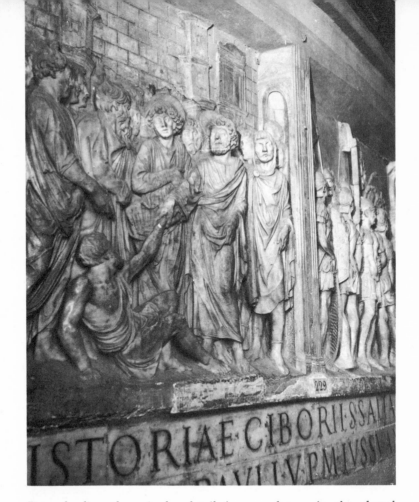

Peter healing the cripple, detail from sculpture in the chapel, St. Peter's.

Third-century sarcophagus of Junius Basus, a Roman consul, crypt of St. Peter's.

(Opposite) Bernini's canopy over St. Peter's tomb.

crypt contains monuments of historical interest in such numbers as would by themselves make any other city famous had it nothing else to show.

Catholics of our country are used, upon entering a church, to take it for granted that the main altar is the altar where the Blessed Sacrament is kept. This, however, is not the Roman usage. Here the main altar is reserved for ceremonial purposes. Indeed in St. Peter's and the other greater Roman churches the main altar is intended only for the Pope or for those specially commissioned to represent him in ceremonies. But in all Roman and Italian churches there is a special chapel in which the Blessed Sacrament is kept. Such is the case in St. Peter's.

In the Sacrament Chapel are two supreme examples of the splendor of marble and carving. The tabernacle, in the form of a little church, is made of gilded bronze and lapis lazuli (one of the rarest and most beautiful of stones). The grand fresco over the altar is a representation of the Blessed Trinity by Pietro da Cortona, an artist of the seventeenth century. On the floor of the chapel is the tomb of Pope Sixtus IV. This bronze tomb is by one of the great artists of the High Renaissance and is much admired as such. It is also interesting in that it was originally a part of the ancient church. But since the pope who began the building of the new St. Peter's was Julius II, a nephew of Pope Sixtus, he caused his uncle's tomb to be placed in his new church. There was to have been a magnificent tomb for Pope Julius also and Michelangelo was to have built it, but he never did. And poor Pope Julius has only a single slab near Pope Sixtus' magnificent bronze. Yet in a way he had his monument, for the greatest of churches, which reflects in its various parts the achievement of many popes for about four and a half centuries, reflects him most of all as the one who began it. And, aside from mortuary monuments, Pope Julius was probably the first pope whose features have been preserved for us in a truly effective portrait. He was painted at least twice by Raphael, and surely these pictures speak. So perhaps Pope Julius did not much need the conventional bronze or marble effigies.

Outside this Sacrament Chapel in a niche in one of the piers is a tomb of very great interest. It is that of the Countess Matilda of Tuscany. In the great battle to keep control of the Church out of the hands of the feudal kings and nobles in the eleventh century, this illustrious woman was one of the chief helpers of the popes in Italy. It was in her castle at Canossa that Pope Gregory VII received the submission of the Holy Roman Emperor Henry IV. This was the high point in a century of struggle which is one of the most glorious of the pages in Church history. The Countess was first buried in Mantua but in 1635 Pope Urban VIII brought her remains to St. Peter's and commissioned Bernini to make the monument. The stately and beautiful woman of the statue is, of course, not a portrait, but it represents what history has to say

Tabernacle in the Blessed Sacrament Chapel, St. Peter's.

Ceiling of the Blessed Sacrament Chapel, St. Peter's.

(Above) Tomb of Pope Innocent VIII.

(Left) Tomb of Countess Matilda.

Tomb of Pope Alexander III.

of her mind and heart. And it is an illustration of how after six centuries Rome still remembered and was grateful.

Two of the most prominent features of St. Peter's are the sepulchral monuments of the popes of recent centuries which are placed in the aisles, transepts, and apse of the basilica, and the statues in heroic size of the founders of religious orders which occupy niches in the nave. Both these groups are a commentary on important phases of the Church's history. The papal tombs are the more interesting, at least artistically, for they also form a commentary on the change of taste in sculpture from the fifteenth century to the twentieth.

The oldest of these statues is that of Innocent VIII who died in 1492. The monument is smaller in scale than most of those in the new church, probably because it was made for the old one. Like that of Sixtus IV in the Sacrament Chapel, it was designed by Pollaiuolo of Florence. Those familiar with Italian art can easily recognize the period in the characteristic sculptural motifs that are known as *quattrocento* (the fourteen hundreds, *i.e.*, the fifteenth century). The monument is not much older than the new church, but it speaks of what to the architects of the new church was an age of the past. Pope Innocent was not one of the greater pontiffs, but his monument brings back to us a period of important events in the background of all of us, the fall of Constantinople, which established four centuries of Moslem control in southeastern Europe; the fall of Granada, which abolished the Moslem faith and culture in the west of Europe; and the discovery of the new world.

Chronologically, the next monument is that of Paul III, located in the apse near the Chair of the Apostle. Pope Paul ended his reign in 1550, just a little over fifty years after Pope Innocent. Artistically this monument is one of the finest in St. Peter's. In style it has moved what might seem centuries away from the *quattrocento* work of Pope Innocent. It was in Pope Paul's reign that the movement sometimes

(Left) Tomb of Pope Clement XIII.

called the Counter Reformation got under way: the Council of Trent was begun by him, the order of the Society of Jesus was founded in his pontificate.

Just opposite is the tomb of Urban VIII, who had so much to do with the completion of the church and with countless buildings throughout Rome which are still in use. One such building is the Church of St. Agnes in Piazza Navona before which is the celebrated Bernini fountain. Pope Urban's reign was just about a century after that of Pope Paul III and here again we note a change of style. Urban's monument was designed by Bernini, the great Baroque master who did the Canopy for him, and it again reflects the ambition of the Baroque to translate sculpture into movement, stone into life.

This movement is carried even further, perhaps to ultimate excess, in the tomb of Alexander VII, the last work of Bernini after he had completed for this pope St. Peter's Colonnade. Except for Michelangelo himself, this great sculptor has left a more powerful impression on St. Peter's than any of the many artists who dealt with the great church. Whether in his own work or in the many works of other artists whom he influenced, the majority of the statues and tombs in the basilica, as well as the Colonnade, the Apostolic Chair, and the majestic baldachin, spring from Bernini.

In due time the Baroque style wore itself out, as all styles will in any art, and late in the eighteenth century a neoclassical style emerged. One of the foremost representatives of this style was Canova. It is to him we owe the tomb of Pope Clement XIII, who reigned just before the days of our American Revolution. The allegorical figure of the Genius of Death has always been admired for its gracefulness, but the real beauty of the monument rises from the noble and recollected figure of the old pope who kneels in prayer.

The tombs of two popes, Benedict XV and Pius XI, carry us forward to our own time. They complete a cycle of history and of art from the late fifteenth century to the middle

(Above) Tomb of Pope Paul III.
(Right) Tomb of Pope Benedict XV.

(Below) Tomb of Pope Pius XI, in white marble, surrounded by gold mosaic.

(Left) The Palatine guard taking guns from the antechamber of the Pope for inspection drill. (Below left) Three Swiss guards on parade. (Below right) A Vatican guard, Olivo Franceschini.

twentieth, and by the events with which they are connected, they show the Church involved at every stage of human history.

Beside St. Peter's is the Palace of the Vatican, which is the residence of the pope, his executive office, an assembly of halls, throne rooms, terraces and pavilions for ceremonial, diplomatic, and other forms of display, a library, an archives, and a museum for the art collection of the Holy See.

The papal palaces are four in number: the Vatican, the Lateran, the Quirinal, and the summer palace at Castel Gandolfo. The last of these has been in active use in recent years as a place of retreat from the heat of the Roman summer. The other three have been the official places of papal residence at different times in history. Just as in Paris, the traveler's memory is embarrassed by the question of which kings lived in the Louvre, on the island, or at the Tuileries, so in Rome you must—for full satisfaction—be able to recall at what periods each of the palaces was in active use as a papal headquarters.

The Lateran—given to the popes by the Emperor Constantine—was the first of these residences. It continued to be

the official residence for about a thousand years. (This is not
true of the present palace, of course, which is only four hundred years old.) The Lateran Palace is venerable to historians
as the center of the Church during about half of her history,
and was the seat of five general councils. After the papal exile
to France in the fourteenth century, large parts were destroyed
by fire and what was left was no longer suitable as a residence.
Following this, for about two centuries the popes dwelt in the
Vatican, during which time the palace acquired most of its
present buildings and the word "Vatican" took on the meaning of the pontifical government, just as "White House" stands
for the presidency of the United States. The Vatican, however,
became more a museum than a residence. So Pope Gregory
XIII, the one who gave us our present calendar, built the
residential palace of the Quirinal. Here the popes lived until
the abolition of the Papal State in 1870, after which the
Quirinal became the residence of the kings of Italy and the
pope returned to the Vatican.

Like all great public buildings, the Vatican needs guards
and caretakers. But in this case the custodians date back to
times when the Vatican was the seat of government of a considerable state, and when their predecessors were the police

and soldiers of that state. Hence their traditional costume and routine are military. The most celebrated and the most striking in appearance are the Swiss Guards. They have retained the helmets and arms which were current in the sixteenth century, and their costume is said to have been designed by Michelangelo. They are actually recruited in the Catholic cantons of Switzerland, from which the first guards were brought by Pope Julius II. They guard the entrance to the Vatican as well as the person of the Holy Father, and they have an honored place in all solemnities and processions at St. Peter's and in the palace.

The Mosaic Factory is a corner of the palace which has much appeal to people who like to see how things are done. The mosaics made here are intended to replace paintings, and the workers thus strive to make as exact copies as possible of the paintings in question, using colorful ceramic particles embedded in cement instead of paint. Originally the work of the factory was for the local needs of the churches, where almost all the paintings have been translated into the mosaic form. But afterward the popes used the factory for the pro-

A seventeen-year-old apprentice drawing out molten rock into sticks for preparation of mosaic stone.

Expert mosaicist in the Vatican workshop with nearly completed work, showing chopped handmade rock and clay on easel.

Mosaic of St. Petronilla.

duction of mosaics that might be used as gifts. Such is the
mosaic copy of the Immaculate Conception by Murillo which
was the gift of the Holy Father to the National Shrine in Washington, D. C. One of the most admired mosaics in St. Peter's
is that of the Entombment of St. Petronilla, which successfully
blends its subordinate colors to enhance the deep blue which is
the dominant.

Rome has been at the center of things for so long a time

that all the possible arts have been practiced there. Perhaps none is more distinctively and peculiarly Roman than the art of the fountains. The city is simply alive with playing water. The riotous and monumental dash of waters playing over the rocks of Trevi, the graceful aerial spurt of the streams in the Esedra, the simple and majestic cascade of the Paolina Fountain on the Janiculum, the playfulness and exquisite grace of the Tortoise Fountain, these are only a few examples of the wild and fairylike imagination with which the Roman artists have treated an element in which this city was so blessed. Everyone remembers the fountains of St. Peter's square, but even within the Vatican courtyards and gardens are still other examples of this art. Two of these are pictured here. They may remind us of the way in which this wonderful church and palace pour out streams of light and beauty. "Hither, as to their fountain, other stars repairing from these golden urns draw light."

Once there was a Rome away from Rome. From about 1309 to 1377 a series of popes lived at Avignon in France, postponing the return to their proper capital because of the civil disorders in Italy. They raised a great Gothic palace there, and it began to look as if the center of the Church might remain there. But Catholic consciousness was too much bound up with Peter's city to be satisfied with Avignon. Finally the force of this feeling compelled the return of the Holy See to its historic home. The Avignon period came to be looked upon as an exile or captivity. Prison òr refuge, the castle of the popes still stands as a memory of one of the strangest of the Church's many strange adventures.

Companion to St. Peter's are the three other major basilicas—St. John Lateran, St. Mary Major, and St. Paul.

The first fact to remember about St. John Lateran is that it is the cathedral of Rome. The tomb of St. Peter and the architectural splendor of his church give most people the impression that this is Rome's cathedral. But this dignity be-

Swiss Guards in their own quarters in Vatican City.

*American Franciscan Sisters of Atonement at their hospice at Assisi.
The spire of the shrine of St. Clare is seen in the background.*

longs to St. John's. It is, therefore, first in rank of all Rome's churches and indeed is given the honor, inscribed on its portico, of being the "mother and head of all the churches of the city and of the world." This honor doubtless goes back to the fact that the palace of the family of Laterani was an imperial residence, was turned over to the pope of the time, and that its church was the first to be built by a Christian emperor. It is even said that in the course of construction Constantine worked at it with his own hands. For all its glory, St. Peter's has never quite caught up with St. John's rank.

The present church, dating from the fourteenth century, is the fourth actual structure, the others having been destroyed by fire and earthquake in the intervening ages. Regrettably its architectural character has been much spoiled. The main altar with its canopy belongs to this fourth church as it was originally built, but the pillars, niches, and other elements of the nave and aisles were covered over in the seventeenth century with some of the least successful of Baroque adornments.

The apse of the cathedral, however, was very beautifully restored under Leo XIII. Here a grand old mosaic brings us back to the Middle Ages as nothing in St. Peter's does. Above the arch is a head of the Saviour, noble and sad in expression, surrounded by winged angels. Beneath this a cross is represented as the source of four streams of water, the symbol of divine grace. At the foot of the hill stags and sheep, signifying human souls, come to drink at the life-giving waters. Our Blessed Lady, Peter, and many others are represented as walking about in the gardens of Paradise. And in the quaint way of the time, the relative importance of these saints is indicated by their size: John the Evangelist being larger than St. Francis or St. Anthony, and these being larger than some contemporary saints who are also represented here. This mosaic makes a splendid study both for its imaginative beauty and for its colorings. And its expressiveness makes us understand how people in those days, who for the most part had

*The fountain Aquilone
in the Vatican gardens.*

Fountain of the Belvidere, Vatican.

Detail of the Trevi fountain, Rome.

no books, could possess considerable culture without reading.

The most venerated shrine in St. John's is the altar of the Blessed Sacrament. The upper structure of the altar is supported on bronze pillars which were donated by Constantine. They had been brought from Jerusalem and their hollow centers were filled with earth from the Holy Land. Above them in gilded bronze is a sculptured Last Supper. Beneath the bronze is a cedar-wood table which has been reverenced for centuries as that upon which our Lord and His apostles ate together on Holy Thursday.

In the apse of St. John's are two monuments, fine in themselves and interesting in this juxtaposition, the tombs of Innocent III and Leo XIII. The reign of Pope Innocent, which ended in 1216, is generally regarded as carrying out in its best practice the theory of medieval society in its close union of civil and religious society. Characteristic of the time was the figure of the crusader, the soldier in the cause of God, which adorns the tomb. Just opposite is the monument of Leo XIII, the pope who in his encyclicals began the enunciation for modern times of the principles of social justice. On this tomb, balancing that of the crusader on Pope Innocent's, we have the figure of the laborer kneeling for the blessing of Pope Leo. If you care to philosophize on history, this is one fine place to do it.

In Rome it would be hard to say how many churches are dedicated to Mary. Certainly there are forty or so which have such historic or artistic interest as to attract the traveler, over and above many which are known only to the Blessed Mother and to them who pray to her. Most outstanding of these churches is called St. Mary Major. Just as St. John Lateran outranks all other churches, so St. Mary Major outranks all churches of our Lady.

Artistically, it is a far finer church than the Lateran. It is also far older and preserves more of its ancient form than any of the four basilicas. The first structure was erected in

Palais des Papes, Avignon, France.

Vatican on the Rhone,
Avignon, France.

352 by Pope Liberius as a result of the fulfillment of his prophetic dream about snow in midsummer. But a century or so later, after the Council of Ephesus had determined the title of our Lady as Mother of God, Pope Sixtus III built a new structure which was essentially the one which we see today. The nave with its long colonnade stands almost as it did fourteen hundred years ago. The mosaics above the columns are very ancient too, much more so than the large one in the apse which itself is contemporaneous with that of the Lateran. Here again we have a wealth of colors and of symbolism. The medieval pilgrim who went from one church to the other had something new to admire and think about and to carry home with him. And so could we, if we would only spend enough time to stop and look at what we see.

The ceiling of the basilica is massively paneled, and the gold used for its adornment was the first gold brought from

America, presented to the Pope by Ferdinand and Isabella as a trophy of the new world.

The great relic of St. Mary's is the cradle of our Lord. This is kept in a magnificent reliquary beneath the high altar. On Christmas morning it is carried in procession and venerated on the altar. At all times it is one of the more important centers of devotion in Rome.

The church has adjoined to it many rich chapels. One of these is that of Our Lady of the Snows which excels among Roman chapels in the magnificence of its marble decoration. The altar is of jasper and lapis lazuli. The columns are of rare and highly wrought marbles. The walls are covered with an elaborate series of paintings which are a sort of artistic *summa* of the Church's doctrines on our Lady and of her glories through the centuries. The chapel, which was built by Paul V, the pope who completed St. Peter's, contains his tomb and that of Clement VIII. Here on August 5 of every year is celebrated the commemoration of the miraculous midsummer snowfall which revealed to Pope Liberius the place where our Lady wished her church to be. At a given moment in the Mass on that day showers of white rose petals are allowed to fall from the dome upon the worshipers.

Main façade of St. John Lateran, Rome.

Chapel of the Blessed Sacrament, St. John Lateran.

On the opposite side of the church, in the Chapel of the Blessed Sacrament, are the tombs of Pius V and Sixtus V. Sixtus V (1585–1590) was one of the most striking figures of the century and has left his mark on Rome as city-planner and restorer. But Pius V (1566–1572), because of his holiness, will appeal more to the Catholic traveler. His canonization took place in 1712 and was until this year of 1954 the last canonization of a pope. His body, clothed in pontifical vestments, is contained in a glass coffin. His face is veiled with a portrait mask of silver. Like Our Lady of the Snows, this chapel is very rich in marbles.

The last of the four basilicas is that of St. Paul. St. Paul Without the Walls is so called because it is situated outside the Wall of Aurelian, which enclosed the city until quite recent times. This wall has an especially interesting history. From

ancient times until the introduction of heavy artillery, it was the practice to make cities safe from siege and brigandage by building high walls around them. In various parts of Rome one can still see fragments of masonry which were parts of the first Roman wall called after King Servius but dating from about four centuries before Christ. At that time Rome, like other cities, needed this protection, but as time went on and her empire began to flourish the capital city grew far beyond the ancient walls. Such was her strength and prestige, indeed, that she needed no more walls for four or five hundred years. Then began the decline. With the invasions of the barbarians, Rome once again needed walls to surround her. So the Emperor Aurelian began the wall, which Gibbon calls a "great but melancholy" structure, and which stood its last of many sieges in 1870. This wall is in large part intact, except where modern traffic has forced breaches. Outside this wall (and therefore outside the ancient city) stands the Basilica of St. Paul Without the Walls.

This isolated position in the rude times after the fall of the Empire left the church in danger. Particularly in the ninth century the open Campagna was subject to raids of Saracen pirates coming up from the sea near Ostia and Anzio. Hence Pope John VIII surrounded the church and the neighboring community with a siege wall and made it a fortified town called Johannopolis (which would be Johnstown). These walls disappeared long ago, but their spirit is still with us.

In the eyes of many tourists, St. Paul's seems more beautiful than St. Peter's. This is at least partly because of its newness and brightness, for the church of today is the very youngest of the great basilicas, having been entirely rebuilt after a fire in the nineteenth century and having been completed only in our own. This church is both magnificent and beautiful, as well as new, but newness and the absence of the dust of centuries, though they have their advantages, cannot replace truly ageless beauty.

St. Mary Major, Rome.

The newness of the present St. Paul's belies its antiquity. In the early part of the fourth century, Constantine, who built St. Peter's and the Lateran, built a small church over Paul's tomb. Fifty years later some of his successors replaced this with a great temple that would be the rival of St. Peter's. This venerable church, restored and enriched from time to time, stood the test of over fourteen hundred years until the fire of 1823. Its destruction, after the love and reverence that had been paid it for so many ages, was taken by the Catholic world as a great tragedy. So appeals were made to Catholics throughout the world to replace it. The result was this grand new structure. Perhaps, if everyone who sees the church would understand that it springs not from the gift of emperors or princes but from the voluntary offerings of Catholics every-

Entrance to St. Paul Without the Walls, Rome.

(Left) Cloister of St. Paul Without the Walls.

(Below) Mosaic apse, St. Paul.

Left) St. Paul, nave.

where, it would be appreciated for more than either its newness or its beauty.

The nave of the church for all its actual newness is, like St. Mary Major's, very ancient in its style and characteristics. Its unbroken files of columns carry the eye forward to the altar and tomb of the apostle. Behind the main columns a second row on either side give depth and magnificence. At the end of the colonnade one sees the Triumphal Arch in mosaic and behind the altar another mosaic similar in character to those in St. Mary Major and the Lateran. These mosaics are remnants saved from the fire which destroyed the old basilica and range in age from high antiquity to the Middle Ages.

Under the high altar and its canopy rest the remains of the Apostle of the Gentiles. Together with Peter he has been honored and revered in Rome for nineteen centuries. It is a solemn thing to come from the shrine of one to the shrine of the other, to contemplate the magnificence of the temples raised to the memory of two men who rose from lowly positions—one a poor fisherman, the other an inconspicuous Roman provincial—to challenge the mind and culture of the world's greatest empire and to begin the process by which this material empire would be succeeded by a spiritual one. The one was great in his rank and upon him was bestowed the divine designation as head of the Church, the other was great by the gift of inspired eloquence and the gift of teaching. Like their Master, both encountered the bitter hatred of the worldly and powerful and went down to earthly death. But like Him, they rose through martydom to life and enjoy that second immortality which comes through the prayer and praise of the Church during sixty generations. All Catholics, indeed all Christians, cannot help but be deeply moved when standing at these holy places and realizing that they are the fountains of all the high faith and ennobling principles which constitute the difference between the Christian and the pagan soul.

St. Paul's for many centuries has been in the custody of Benedictine monks, and there is no monastic cloister more exquisite than St. Paul's unless it be that of the Lateran. Here among the graceful columns of twisted marble, the hedges and the grass, rise the spirit of serenity and the contemplation of high and great thoughts that made this place a refuge and a gathering place of strength to such souls as Hildebrand. Once a monk of St. Paul's, Hildebrand lived during the eleventh century—the halfway point of the Church's long history. He was the impulse and the guide for the struggles with a secularizing spirit which threatened to pervert the Church. He was for most of his years a battler and contender, and when he died in 1085 as Pope Gregory VII he died in exile and defeat. But he never lost the consciousness of purpose which he had gathered in the cloister. And we can imagine how in peaceful moments at the shrine of the apostle or in meditation as he walked under these arches he learned the spirit that make the confessor and the martyr.

In our time we have seen the deaths of kings; most of those who remain are reduced to carrying on with little more than the ceremonial traditions of monarchy. Only the Papacy emerges in the din and turmoil of this century as holding from the past and administering with efficacy in the present the authority to which it was appointed in the beginning. And it may be questioned whether age for age any dynasty of kings has approached this one in the frequency with which greatness of mind paralleled the importance of position. It is to the divine guidance which has continued to bless that which was divinely established that we owe this happy confluence. In the history of kings the phenomenon of personal greatness has been rare, in the history of the popes it has been frequent. And we may add that our own generation has seen a time as rich as any in that leadership and in the assertion, in a very material world, of the primacy of the spiritual.

ITALY

PERHAPS THERE IS NO COUNTRY IN THE world which has been so much loved by those who do not belong to it as Italy. In the past the love has taken the form of using violence to possess it. Lamentation for this fact pervades Italian literature and finds its most striking expression in Alfieri's sonnet in which he wishes that his country had been either stronger to repel or less beautiful to attract those whose love crushed her to death. But aside from the conquerors there were always the pilgrims and sojourners, and all European literatures reflect the strange and inimitable power given to this land to dwell as a queen in the imagination of the world.

> Open my heart and you will see
> Graved inside of it, "Italy."
> Such lovers old are I and she,
> So it always was, so shall ever be.

Franciscan students in prayer before the tomb of St. Francis of Assisi.

49

So wrote Browning, and his love was reflected in much more than this one poem. His lines might serve to express the feeling of the millions who before and after his time have felt that this was the fairest indeed of all the countries they have beheld.

We have seen the part played in this by Rome, which has remained a center of universal interest longer than any other city and still remains such a center. But the charm belongs to the whole of the magic land. Returning after eighteen years, one traveler told of how his heartbeat quickened with emotion as he came over the frontier at Ventimiglia and saw once more the little cities—masses of gray wall and red roof and exquisite campanili among the pines and olives—tumbling down the rocks into the purple sea. Or again how the frescoes in Spoleto or San Gemignano made him feel once more the sheer, massive, overpowering gift of creating beauty with which the people of this country have endowed all posterity. Or again when he saw Giotto's campanile against the sunset "a mass of mountain alabaster, carved like a sea shell and colored like a morning cloud," or when Siena's archway proclaimed in its ancient inscription that she opened her heart to him even more than she did her gateway, or when the fairyland fountains of the Clitumnus murmured among the cypress and willows the song they had sung to Pliny long ago, or when Ravenna in her lonely fenland carried him back in her mosaics to the coruscating splendor of the Byzantine age, or when the cities of the Emilian plain—Parma, Piacenza, Modena—brought him in fancy to the fair dawn when Europe woke "to find herself clothed in the white vesture of churches"—the revisiting of all these scenes made him bow with gratitude before the benefactions of the centuries.

The direct devotional interest of each Catholic shrine must be considered topically, for it follows no pattern. But it may help those whose historical recollections have become blurred to do a little refocusing; let us then rough out Italian history in blocks of centuries, sacrificing exactitude to simplicity.

1. Christianity came almost immediately to Italy in the person of the two great apostles, Peter and Paul, and their coadjutors. For nearly three hundred years it met with the resistance of the official Roman mind. It grew against that resistance, and with the Emperor Constantine in 311 came the end of persecution.

2. For the better part of two more centuries (the fourth and fifth) Italy continued to be governed in some sense by the now Christian emperors. But these rulers lived at Constantinople and the city of Rome was only nominally the capital. During this period the popes became, if not the rulers of Rome, at least the receivers of much of the responsibilities of government which the ostensible rulers could not or would not exercise.

3. For three more centuries (sixth, seventh, and eighth) Italy became an object of struggle between the viceroys of the eastern emperors and the very much more vigorous generals of the barbarians, notably of the Ostrogoths and Lombards. (The latter have given their name to one of the most important of the Italian provinces.) During these centuries, in their position as bishops of Rome, the popes, of whom the most important was Gregory the Great (590–604), became in fact, though not yet in law and title, the civil rulers of central Italy. The foundations of the papal monarchy were laid.

4. In the ninth century Charlemagne was crowned at Rome as Holy Roman Emperor and, with the power of the position, attempted to bring to Europe peace and order through the revival of the Christian empire. The idea of a united Europe, although it failed, continued to be the policy and dream of the next five centuries. The attempt to implement the dream always took the form of capturing and ruling from a throne in Rome. One of the most important factors in the failure (apart from any inherent difficulties in the lack of

*San Miniato al Monte, on the sum-
mit of a hill in Florence.*

Choir stalls, San Miniato.

Nave and choir of San Miniato.

means) was the irreconcilability of the Imperial policy with the determination of the Church not to be made subservient to Caesar. Caesar, in order to obtain the laudable aim of peace and order, always seemed to find it necessary to adopt the means of laying hands upon the Church. This led to the wars of Papacy and Empire which went on from the eleventh to the middle of the thirteenth century and which ended in the final defeat of the German emperors in the person of Frederick II.

5. The fourteenth and fifteenth centuries are marked by the rise of the Italian city-states. Florence, Pisa, Genoa, Milan, Venice, and many others acquired a sovereignty over the neighboring countrysides and smaller towns. Each of these "republics" was at first ruled by a senate of merchants, professional men, and soldiers. Gradually single individuals established personal control and the "republics" fell under the rule of great dynastic families. Such were the Medici in Florence or the Visconti in Milan. Genoa and Venice, however, which wielded considerable sea power, were ruled by boards of merchant princes with doges at their head. Simultaneously in Rome the popes reestablished and enlarged the papal monarchy.

6. Three centuries (the sixteenth to the nineteenth) were characterized by the ascendancy of foreign powers, notably of Spain and Austria, over the Italian principalities. During this time the Papacy continued to control the Papal State of central Italy, although it was in frequent conflict with Spain, with Austria, and with others.

7. The nineteenth century opened with the rise of Napoleon and continued to ferment with the ideas of the French Revolution, which eventually inspired the *Risorgimento* (Revival) and, in less direct ways, caused the establishment of the Kingdom of Italy under the House of Savoy. This movement forcibly terminated the papal monarchy in 1870.

8. World War I, followed by the disorders of communism and socialism, brought about the movement known as Fascism.

World War II, in which Italy was defeated, saw the downfall of both the monarchy and the Fascist order. The latter, however, left a valuable legacy to the future in the reestablishment of papal independence in the form of a small state in an extra-territorial Vatican City. This situation, accepted by the Holy See in the Concordat of 1929, has survived the war and has already proved its worth to civil society in Italy and elsewhere by the fact that the Holy See has worked with the non-communist and civilized nations, particularly the United States, in fending off the communist threat. The Italian Republic has had no better ally in maintaining the integrity of its threatened order than the tiny Vatican state which, under changed form, continues the tradition begun in the sixth century under the leadership of Gregory I.

The various periods mentioned in this brief retrospect are often characterized by the type of buildings which they erected, particularly by the churches, which were, after all, centers of culture and religion. During the first period there was little opportunity to erect buildings. However, the substructure of San Clemente in Rome dates back to those apostolic times when the early Christians gathered in whatever type of edifice was available to them.

The second period is reflected principally in the style which is called Basilican or Early Christian. This was shown in the nave of St. Mary Major; a modern revival of it was St. Paul's Without the Walls.

The third period, carrying on the Basilica structure, is remarkable for the development of mosaic. The classic center of this wonderful art was the Byzantine capital in Italy, Ravenna.

The fourth period, from the ninth to the thirteenth century, saw the development of Romanesque and, afterward, of Gothic architecture. The Romanesque flourished most widely in Italy in its more amiable and graceful adaptation known as the Lombard style. The lovely campanili or bell towers, which are such an important feature in the Italian landscape, are prevailingly from this period or influenced by it. And the wonderful churches at Lucca, at Pisa, at Spoleto, at Piacenza—each adorned with rich and gracious arcades—are examples of what the Italians could do to lighten and brighten the solemn and somewhat heavy grandeur of the northern Romanesque.

The Italians also put their hands to the Gothic and achieved some wonderful results at Siena, Orvieto, Milan, and elsewhere. Venice contributed a strange amalgam of the Gothic and Byzantine, and Florence experimented with the Gothic in her cathedral and in Sante Croce. But all these great churches, however wonderful, are really aberrations from the true line of Gothic. No one who has seen the Gothic of France, or England, or even of Spain, will feel that Italy was one of its real homes.

The fifth period, that of the Italian republics and despots, was one in which Greek and Roman art and architecture influenced builders and artists of every craft to adapt a style that was so rich that, with modifications, it has lived on to our own time. The new type of building became the dwelling place of new types of painting and sculpture. Simultaneously a rich polyphonic development of music superimposed itself upon the simpler musical foundation of the medieval church. The original and high Renaissance was interrupted by the invention of the Baroque. The simplicity and grandeur of a church like San Lorenzo in Florence was succeeded by the restless and imaginative vigor of such a one as the Gesù in Rome or as St. Peter's itself. This movement had its final moments of excess and then yielded place to the familiar Neoclassic.

Studying history in buildings makes both history and buildings more vivid. In Italy this approach is especially of value since here is a continuous sequence of building—from the very old to the very new.

One of the finest of the churches built in the eleventh

century is San Miniato al Monte. The hill on which it stands is a sort of suburb of Florence. There was a great abbey here nine hundred years ago, one of the largest and most influential in Tuscany. Long before the great days of the Renaissance, when all Europe was beginning its architectural awakening, this venerable and chastely beautiful church became one of the heralds of that rebirth. It stands today in all of its original character.

In connection with this church two people must be remembered. One is Michelangelo. It has already been related how he paused on the terrace before San Miniato when he was leaving for Rome and said good-by to Brunelleschi's dome. The terrace of the church is now named for him, and it is a splendid place in which to read the preface to George Eliot's *Romola*.

The other person is St. John Gualberti, founder of the order of Vallombrosa. In the days when the church was new, he—a Florentine monk—feuded with the members of another family. In passing behind San Miniato one day he came upon one of these enemies, who was unarmed. In accordance with the code of the time, John was about to kill him. But the man fell at his feet and spread his arms in the form of a cross, and John forgave him. Dismissing him, John went into the church to pray. The story goes that the figure of the Crucified bowed its head to salute him for his act of Christian mercy and that this was the beginning of his path to sainthood.

Across the city of Florence on the slope of another hill lies the city of Fiesole, one of the oldest in Italy and the parent, it is said, of Florence herself. Two places here are of special interest to Americans, not because they are celebrated places of pilgrimage but as examples of how the living Church of the twentieth century is paying back its debt to the past, and of how the Catholics of English-speaking lands bring back to Italy some return for what she has given. One of these is the Rest House of the English and Irish Sisters of the Little

The Honorable Mrs. Clare Boothe Luce, United States Ambassador to Italy, visits the Villa Schifanoia

Shrine in the woods at the Villa Schifanoia, Florence.

Nostra Signora della Guardia, Genoa.

Company of Mary—the Blue Nuns, as so many residents of Florence know them. The other is the Villa Schifanoia (whose name means "Get away from Bother"). This beautiful place was the property of The Hon. Myron Taylor, presidential representative to the Holy See. Mr. Taylor made it over to the Holy See, which put it to use by summoning here a group of Dominican sisters from Sinsinawa, Wisconsin. It is to be hoped that the young women who study here will get much and give much in international understanding and in the deepening of Christian culture.

Predominant in Italian veneration of the saints is the devotion to the Madonna. Seemingly everywhere it is possible to come across some regional shrine with its festa, its statue or Byzantine image, its processions, its tradition of miraculous intervention to heal the troubles or to rebuke the sinfulness of men. Each little hill town with its church dedicated to the Assunta or the Addolorata, each provincial pilgrimage church like our Lady of Pompeii or the Sanctuary of Oropa in the Alps of Piedmont, each great cathedral like Santa Maria del Fiore in Florence focused in past times the devotion of that region and focuses in this much traveled time more or less of the attention of the world.

Genoa also has a shrine of our Lady, watching over the sea. It is not one of the greater churches, as you can see, and not what you might expect of Genoa "the Proud." But it draws the faith and love of people, and in any case, some of the Madonna's trophies, even in Italy, may be left to the future.

The most celebrated shrine of our Lady in Italy and, before the apparitions at Lourdes, the most celebrated in the world, is the Basilica of Loreto. This town, named from a laurel grove which was once here, is the location of the Holy House of Nazareth. According to a tradition prevalent since

Souvenir stand outside Nostra Signora della Guardia.
Strings of nuts are traditional souvenirs.

the fifteenth century this is the original house which was used by the Holy Family at Nazareth. It is said that it was miraculously carried off by angels and, after stopping elsewhere for a short time, came to rest here near the Adriatic. The devotion which sprang up was so great as to require a large church. So here, as at Assisi, a monumental shrine encloses and protects a little rustic dwelling that has fascinated all peoples with a Catholic culture who love the thought of our Lord in association with His mother because it seems to illuminate the central facts of their own lives with a divine sanction and blessing.

I remember standing on the terrace in front of the Cathedral of Milan. On the bronze portals are small panels representing scenes in the life of our Lord. One of the scenes, the Nativity, is at eye level. A young couple, probably farmers visiting the city, came to look and, as they were about to go, the man and then the woman reverently kissed the little bronze infant in the manger. It is this feeling, alive in millions of

hearts, that makes such a place as the shrine at Loreto mean so much.

Italy has given to the world many great names and many saints. Perhaps she has given none who has been more a saint or who has had more power to make the world see the beauty of holiness than Francis of Assisi. We have brought together here a number of photographs of Assisi in the hope of carrying to the reader some of the serene and heavenly atmosphere which is St. Francis' legacy to the city of his birth and life and death. Over one of the city portals there is painted his blessing to Assisi. A visitor does not, of course, know the citizens in their daily lives, but one likes to think that the blessing of St. Francis has effect among them. Surely one sees nothing in this lovely place to mar the "Franciscan" impression that it so strongly conveys.

The great church of Assisi is the Church of the Conventuals ("Black" Franciscan) at the west end of the town. It is a

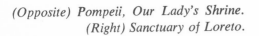
(Opposite) Pompeii, Our Lady's Shrine.
(Right) Sanctuary of Loreto.

One of the main gates in the city wall of Assisi.

monumental structure, built like a three-storied castle out on the shoulder of a hill. It was built as a monument over the tomb of the saint. The saint was buried in rough stone deep in the earth, but about a century ago the place was opened and the present crypt chapel built so that people might come close, as they love to do, and be in touch with the very tomb.

Such a large church was not needed to be merely a burial place, however; it was built to house the great number of the

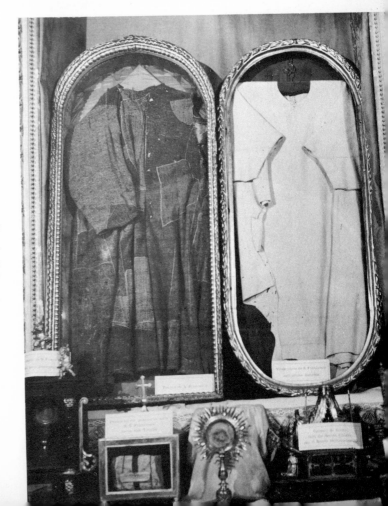

(Above, right) Handwriting of St. Francis of Assisi. (Right) Garments of St. Francis, including his gray home-spun habit and cowl, the white woolen tunic worn during his last illness, and sandals made for him by St. Clare.

lovers of St. Francis and to be, as it were, a museum for the gifts of the generations.

The first such gift was probably the noblest. For the paintings here by Cimabue and Giotto are the tribute of the very glorious dawn of Italian art. Painting, which was for so many centuries rigid and conventional, became free with Giotto. This great man's gifts were exercised here (as at Padua for the story of our Lord) to celebrate the varied and beautiful scenes in the history and legend of St. Francis.

Two relics preserved here are exceptionally moving. One is a parchment written on by St. Francis himself with the words, ordered in Franciscan playfulness: "May the Lord bless, brother Leo, thee." The other is the habit of St. Francis—rough, worn, and patched as he always wore it from the day when he renounced the possessions of his family. As Chesterton says, it was only ten years before this became the costume of five thousand men, and in another century the great Dante wore it when he was carried to his grave.

One of the things that go to make up the strange and complicated beauty of the Franciscan story is the love the saint had for God's creatures in the ranks inferior to man. So the Franciscan monastery abounds in flowers and gardens, and doves have a place here because of St. Francis' protection of them. Another characteristic was the association of religion with gaiety rather than with grimness. It will please St. Francis' friends to see how his novices of today are trained in ways that are compatible with the Franciscan happiness.

Lastly there is St. Clare's church, not her little convent of San Damiano down the hill, which St. Francis gave her when he left for the Porziuncola, but the church raised as a monument over her tomb. It is a Gothic church of the thir-

A section of the Giotto paintings in the Basilica.

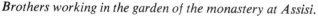
Brothers working in the garden of the monastery at Assisi.   *Novices bowling.*

teenth century. In a way it is very dim and dark. But perhaps there is no church where the beautiful stained-glass windows are so bright and gemlike as here. It seems suggestive of the soul shutting itself off in the cloister from human sight and sounds so that it may gaze through apertures upon the heavenly light.

Sharing the company of St. Francis in popular devotion is his disciple, St. Anthony. St Anthony is called "of Padua," although he was born in Portugal. But his birthplace is often forgotten because he did so much for the people of Padua, the place where he ended his life and where his relics lie. Here again a Gothic church, very picturesque and of enormous proportions, is the monument which houses the tomb. The tomb chapel, one of very great beauty, dates from about 1550, the

Interior cloister with statue of St. Francis.

Church of St. Clare at Assisi.

*Franciscan brother with pet pigeon of
the order.*

time of the High Renaissance. Rich reliefs in gilded bronze adorn it. Various paintings represent the miracles of St. Anthony. One, particularly quaint, represents the story from the Little Flowers of St. Francis telling how St. Anthony talked to the fishes because the people would not listen to his sermon and how the fishes came to the shore and arranged themselves in rows, the smaller ones in front, to hear him, and how they waved their fins to applaud him. Perhaps, were the good saint living today, he might feel like giving this sermon again, for he must be kept so busy listening to the petitions of people who are continually talking to him and telling him what they want him to do that he gets no chance to talk to them of the truth and the glories of the Lord. On the other hand, now that he is in Paradise, perhaps he sees the troubles of earth too clearly to be annoyed with the insistence of the confused, the agitated, the forlorn. The Church builds these great palace churches and tombs of bronze and marble, and gives access to them for people who otherwise would not have the uses of magnificence, so that some drops of comfort and solace may fall on them from the place where our heavenly Father holds for them the treasures that do not rust or waste. Perhaps the combination is of the best when St. Anthony does kind things for us and St. Francis teaches us how to be kind to others.

(Left) Brass-bronze relief of the entombment at St. Anthony's.   *(Right) Padua, St. Anthony's Shrine.*

The Basilica of St. Anthony of Padua.

Another shrine which attracts much attention is that of the Holy Shroud in Turin. This relic of the winding sheet in which our Lord was buried was brought here from the east and has been venerated here since the sixteenth century. It has been beautifully housed behind the altar and surrounded with all the wealth of decoration that could be given it. A great deal has been written about this relic in recent years, especially since it was discovered that the marks of sweat and blood on the shroud are such as to constitute a photographic phenomenon which cannot be explained except on the supposition of the relic's authenticity. There is an extensive literature

69

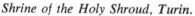

Shrine of the Holy Shroud, Turin.　　*Chapel of the Holy Shroud, Turin.*

of discussion. But if you have not time to read it, you may instead find time to think more of what our Lord did for us, and to pray, in the words of the *Stabat Mater,* that "such great labor be not in vain."

Three shrines of particular magnificence in Italy are at Siena, Pavia, and Venice.

Siena's cathedral, like that of the mother cathedral of the United States, at Baltimore, is dedicated to the Assumption. We have said before that the Italians did not seem to feel too happy with the Gothic. When they did take to it they did so on their own terms and acted with it in ways that are not approved by Gothic enthusiasts or by critics generally. However, in so doing they achieved something magnificent and something which delights the modern traveler. It delighted the thirteenth century Sienese too, for they had scarcely finished this grand edifice when they decided to make it just the arm or transept of another church, which was begun but never finished. Had they gone on they might have been building to the present day, for the scale was such as to have made it the largest church in the world. The Black Death, the plague of 1348, which changed so many things in medieval Europe, changed the minds of the Sienese.

However, there is much left to be proud of: the façade made of many marbles and glowing with mosaic; the unique

70

pavement of inlaid marbles, so precious that it has to be kept covered except on special occasions; the noble pulpit by Pisano; and a wilderness of painting and sculpture. In addition to all this is the library of the cathedral containing the frescoes of the life of Pope Pius II by Pinturicchio.

At the close of the fourteenth century the Visconti family, in the person of its Duke Gian Galeazzo Visconti, governed from Milan and was in process of extending its control through much of northern and central Italy. All the great despotic families were lovers of magnificence, and this one—no exception—came close to outbidding all the rest by erecting the Carthusian monastery church at Pavia. (Called *Certosa* in Italian, monasteries of this order are familiar to us by the French name of *Chartreuse* and the English *Charterhouse*.)

If you visit the original home of the Carthusians in the Alpine solitudes near Grenoble you will find vastness but neither architectural ornament nor luxury. But at Pavia monastic simplicity yielded to the pressure of the Renaissance love of splendor. The church reflects an unusual combination of architecutural styles: Romanesque, Gothic, Renaissance, and even, in some of its altars, the Baroque. But somehow they are blended together in a synthesis of grandeur. We are becoming accustomed to that something at the opposite end of the architectural scale, called "Contemporary." If we get tired easily, and some of us do, of the "contrast by masses," the "functional," and above all the pseudo-functional, it would be a relief to make a retreat of an hour or so at the Certosa. But perhaps the good Carthusians, who are so heavily cloistered that they do not even give retreats, and who are rated to have the most severe rule in the Catholic Church, would refer you in sign language to orders like the Trappists, which have a slightly more sociable austerity.

Perhaps the Pavian masterpiece is too far at the other end of art from the Contemporary. So for our last Italian picture we have taken a marvel of design—Santa Maria della

Siena, the Cathedral.

*Santa Maria della Salute,
Venice.*

Salute at Venice, which holds an exquisite balance between the magnificent and the stately. We could not perhaps call the design simple, but the complicated elements are mingled with such a perfect subordination of parts that it is really one of the architectural marvels of the world.

Like all the Italian wonders, it reflects faith and devotion. The church was built in the seventeenth century in fulfillment of a vow made at a time of pestilence. The plague ended and health (*la salute*) returned. Hence it is called Our Lady of Health. It sounds poor in English and so let us return to its beautiful Italian name, Santa Maria della Salute.

Our Lady has not exhausted her resources when we leave Italy. But somehow or other it is hard to find any other country which has used so many forms of praise in her honor or spoken of her with more of the eloquence of beauty and of love.

(Opposite) Façade of the Certosa at Pavia.
(Below) The large cloister of the Certosa.
(Right) The small cloister.

FRANCE

IF ITALY SEEMS TO BE THE MOST BELOVED OF
European countries then it might be said
that France is the most admired. In recent centuries, and up
at least to the threshold of our own time, any ideas or manners
or styles that got around the world generally were likely to
spread in a French form. There has been no city which has
greater claim than Paris to be the cultural capital of the world.

What is true of France in the recent general history of the
world has been true for many centuries in the record of
Christendom. The reader of Church history finds himself more
engaged with France with every century into which he advances. Rome is the capital, the center of Catholicism, and has
always had an outpouring of genius and of sanctity, but somehow the important people of Italy had a way of getting involved with France, as will be suggested by the mere mention
of names like Patrick, Columbanus, Becket, Anselm, Aquinas.
At one moment, as we saw, the pull of forces was so great that

Paris, apse of Notre Dame.

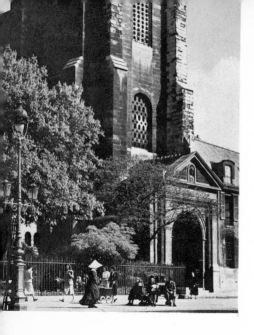

St. Germain des Près, the oldest working church in Paris.

the popes kept their court in France for seventy years. When the tide of the Moslem power was rising in the seventh century it was checked and turned back in France. When the force of the Protestant revolt threatened to engulf Catholicism its most critical defeat was sustained in France. The holy name of Francis (which means Frenchman) was first used by an Italian father who gave it to his son. In France the greatest of Italian poets had some of his deepest experience. The most powerful artistic expression of the Christian genius, Gothic architecture, had its origin in France and found its most perfect expression there.

The royal apse of Notre Dame in Paris is, therefore, a fitting introduction to our chapter on the shrines of France. Remarkable for its architectural originality, it is also remarkable for the commanding situation in which it is placed, like some fantastic ship of stone sailing upon the Seine.

Near the spot where this photograph was taken is a statue that should be known to all who are interested in our book, the statue of the patroness of Paris, St. Genevieve. In the fifth century, when the old imperial government was breaking down and the citizens of France were confronted with the Germanic invasions, it often fell to individual inspiration to

St. Séverin, Paris.

assume the burden of organizing resistance. This was done by many a bishop and by many a monastery. In this time it was done by a woman whose natural gifts were enhanced by the ascendancy of sanctity. On two occasions she led the citizens of Paris and upheld their courage in time of siege. On another occasion she obtained such diplomatic terms from the conquering Clovis as to pave the way for the peaceful foundation of the Frankish kingdom. This statue rising from a pier of the bridge shows her as a stately woman protecting the boy (the city of Paris) who stands before her and looks up river as if to the places whence came the barges bringing relief to the invested city. It is a gracious and noble tribute of modern France to one of the builders of her greatness. In sight of the apse of Notre Dame, it is also an evidence of the survival into our day of the religious faith that has been at the heart of French civilization through the ages.

Paris is not as rich in ancient churches as might be expected. But two are of considerable interest, being among the oldest still in use. St. Germain des Prés dates in part from eight hundred years ago. St. Séverin is somewhat younger, being of the Gothic time. It is very weathered in its appearance but its architectural features are particularly well preserved. It is not merely a museum piece but an active parish in a quarter of Paris which is very populous but which has much of the atmosphere of past times.

It is usually said that the four greatest French cathedrals are those of Paris, Amiens, Rheims, and Chartres. Of these the most admired is probably Chartres. For one thing it is blessed with a fine situation. Commanding the skyline of the town, it can be seen for many miles across the flat country of La Beauce. Its towers, built three centuries apart and quite dissimilar in structure, have some kind of harmony that cannot be analyzed. There is no shock of incongruity at the intrusion of modern industrialism, a thing which does so much to destroy the beauty of Rouen, for example. Seen from a dis-

Chartres, the cathedral.

Sculpture detail, St. Theodore, Chartres.

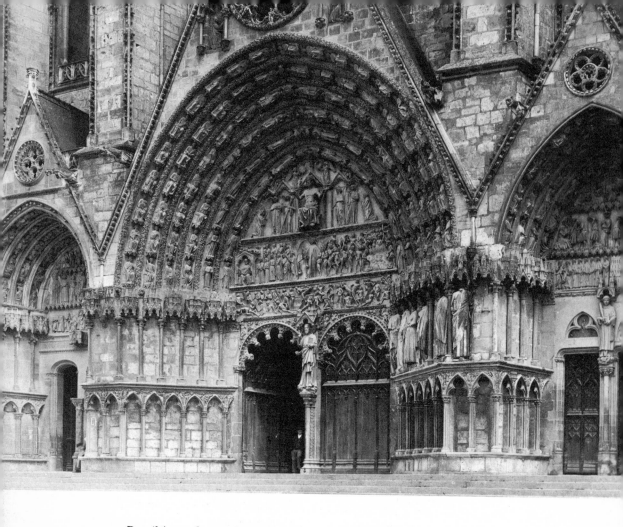

Detail from the portico, Bourges.   *Front façade of the cathedral at Laon.*

tance the city might still be that of centuries ago. The country-side is pure country, very silent and peaceful. There are few Gothic masterpieces which enjoy this privilege of bringing you into the atmosphere of dream.

Inside the church there is the miracle of glass. In this Chartres outranks the others. Readers of Henry Adams will remember his wonderful analysis of the meaning of these windows as a kind of wall of beauty raised to contain the court of the Queen of Heaven.

thedral at Bourges.

Bourges has the largest of the cathedrals after the four just mentioned. It is also one of the finest, its porches being very rich in medieval sculpture. That of Laon is also famous for the size and boldness of its four towers and for the majesty of its nave. It was in the line of fire in the two great wars, but it did not suffer the tragic fate which befell Rheims in the first war and Rouen in the second.

Tours has a fine cathedral dedicated to St. Gatien, its

oir and nave of Laon, showing Romanesque-style pillars.

U.S. Air Force men visit Laon.

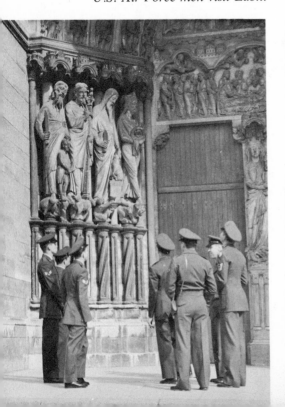

Tours, Cathedral of St. Gatien.

first bishop. But the name of the city is more often connected with St. Martin, one of the greatest saints of France. In his time (he died in 397) there was need of an apostolate in the countryside. While the cities were already converted to Christianity, the countrysides in France and Italy were slow to accept the faith, perhaps because the preachers of the faith were slow to come to them. The name "pagan" originally meant "countryman." But since city people were Christian and countrymen non-Christian, the word came to have the meaning which it has for us. In another form, "peasant," it retains its ancient meaning.

This state of things was changed by an active apostolate in the fourth century, of which St. Martin was the outstanding representative. He combined this mission with the life of a monk, so that he is also the founder of the monastic tradition in France. These facts, and the fame of miracles, made his name very much beloved even unto our own time. We Americans hear little about him, but everyone who has felt the charm of the French landscape, whether in some actual place or in some picture like "The Angelus," has reason to be grateful to St. Martin who made the pagan Christian in these lovely fields long before the village spires arose and the bells sounded from them.

The town of Caen is associated with the Norman dukes who became kings of England and straddled the channel with their power after the battle of Hastings in 1066. These great rulers were also great builders. In Caen they raised two abbey churches, one for women and one for men. These two abbeys are among the most admired examples of the stark, fortresslike Romanesque that is so expressive of that iron time and of its strong and simple faith. One of the finest pages in history is that which relates the story of these strange and wonderful people. Coming to France as pirates from Scandinavia, they settled in the section to which they have given their name of Normandy. In two centuries they made their military power

Caen, Abbaye aux Hommes.

Lantern of Notre Dame de la Grande, Poitiers.

felt in every country from Ireland to Palestine. But they also left in each place a deep impress of their imposing gifts of culture. Caen takes us back to the beginning of all this with its massive simplicity and power.

Also Romanesque, but without simplicity, are Notre Dame la Grande at Poitiers, where the façade is notable for the richness of its ornamentation, and Vézelay, the Burgundian abbey church of the Madeleine. Here the Romanesque passes into the Gothic before your eyes, as the round arched nave gives place to the pointed chancel.

Vézelay is another church fortunate in its location. A village climbs about the upper part of a hill. The church stands on a terrace at the top and can be seen for great distances from every point of the compass. The original abbey, founded in the tenth century, became famous because of the relics of Mary Magdalen that were brought to it from Provence at a time when the Saracens were menacing the south of France.

84

The place became a center of pilgrimage frequented by multitudes. So famous was it that St. Bernard chose it in 1142 to announce the Second Crusade. On the slope below the village he exhorted the assembly to support the movement. From here he went about France and Germany arousing Christendom to another effort to save the Holy Land.

The figure of St. Bernard dominates the history of Church and State in the first part of the twelfth century in an extraordinary way. This great Burgundian and the Cistercian order of which he was the leading spirit, though not the founder, are an instance of the great influence of France in Church history

Portal of St. Pierre de la Tour at Aulnay near Poitiers.

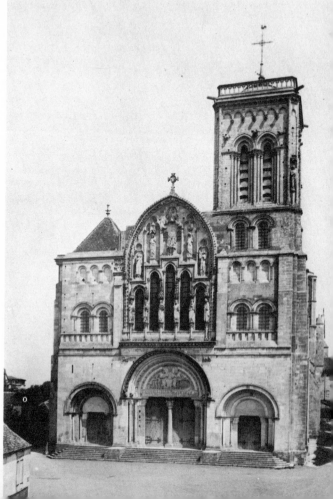

(Above) St. Bernard. (Above right) Cistercian monks meditate in the chapter house of the abbey at Sénanque.

of which we spoke. Like St. Martin eight centuries before him, he blended the almost contradictory qualities of monk and reformer, of contemplative and apostle. His spiritual writings are of such depth and beauty as to suggest a life completely dedicated to the cloister. Yet there were few who traveled more, urged as he was by call after call to settle the grave issues which disturbed western Christendom in his time. In 1953 his seventh centenary was celebrated at Vézelay, Dijon, and elsewhere. In connection with this celebration, two large maps were displayed in the Dijon Museum, one to illustrate the extent of his journeys and the other to show the great number of Cistercian foundations made in his lifetime. When we think of the difficulties of travel in those days we cannot suppress our surprise. It is one of the junctures of history that makes us realize the tremendous effort that it took in past times just to hold civilization together. The spread of the Cistercian monasteries meant just that. An organized force was created to unite the efforts and the aims of those who represented the higher spiritual interests of Europe—in other words its conscience. The individual monasteries of the Benedictine Rule existed so that men of high spiritual ideals might come together and protect the ideals from being thwarted. But the orders, first of Cluny and then of Citeaux, were in effect unions of monasteries so that the strength of the spiritual might be one and work to one end for the Church all over the continent.

In after centuries the work of these earlier orders was eclipsed by the mendicant orders of the thirteenth century and again by the strongly organized groups formed to combat the Protestant revolt. But the ideal of the contemplative continued to exist. The Cistercians live the life of prayer at Citeaux, their original home in Burgundy, and in many other parts of France. We have here a picture of one of the monasteries at Sénanque where the strength of the Cistercian purpose is illustrated by its continuance after eight centuries.

87

Vézelay, Church of the Madeleine.

Notre Dame of Strasbourg, Notre Dame of Dijon, and St. Cecilia of Albi complete the group of the greater individual churches. Together they represent principally the thirteenth century, but a comparison of the photographs will suggest the variety and individuality that was possible within the Gothic pattern. The cathedral at Albi is particularly striking for its blend of the ecclesiastical with the military. It reminds us of the time when feudalism had atomized society to the point where every town had its own fortifications and where, in some cases, even churches had to be ready to maintain their defense against freebooters. The church of Les Saintes Maries (the Holy Marys) is another example of this fortification. It is a shrine dedicated to the two saints named Mary who were said to have come to Provence with Magdalen and Martha and Lazarus. The quaint little sculpture shows them in their boat

Strasbourg, view of the cathedral across the courtyard of the château.

carrying with them, perhaps, the ointments that they had carried to the tomb on the morning of the Resurrection.

We have frequently mentioned, with reference to many of these churches, the advantage of their location. In this particular there is no church in France or elsewhere which rejoices in a finer site than the Basilica of Notre Dame de la Garde at Marseilles. Five hundred feet above the city it looks out over the buff houses and red roofs to the harbor and the sea. The church was built in 1864 and, therefore, belongs with Fourvières at Lyons and with Sacré Coeur in Paris to the offerings which the nineteenth century made to God and our Lady. That century was a great one, but was not at its best in architecture. Neither the strength nor the simplicity of the Middle Ages survived in it. But, pending the return to better ways of building, Notre Dame de la Garde had at least the

Dijon, façade of Notre Dame.   *Albi, Cathedral of St. Cecilia.*

Les Saintes Maries de la Mer.

beauty of being the gift of generous hearts, and the sublimity
of the scenery constitutes an atmosphere of spiritual elevation,
of contemplation, and of prayer.

In the Middle Ages the name of LePuy was known all over
Europe because of the shrines of the Bessed Virgin there. The
pilgrimages rivaled those of Rome and Compostela in numbers.
And a very long list is given of people famous in Church and
State who came there. At least four of the popes prayed there.
One of them, Clement IV, had been Bishop of LePuy. It was
from LePuy that Urban II in 1095 wrote the letters of summons
to the Council of Clermont at which the First Crusade was
launched. Beginning with Charlemagne, who made it twice,
many of the kings of France made the pilgrimage. St. Louis IX
also came twice. On one occasion he met the King of Aragon at
the shrine. Notable also are the visits of great saints, of whom
we may mention St. Dominic, St. Vincent Ferrer, St. Anthony
of Padua, and St. John Francis Regis. Particularly touching is

the recollection that in 1429 a woman from a little house in Domremy came as a pilgrim. It was the year when Joan of Arc had set out on her strange and wonderful and tragic mission; the pilgrim was her mother, who doubtless came here to set at rest her anxieties and to gain strength for the ordeal of the next two years.

Parenthetically it may be hoped that France will yet build what should prove to be one of her most beautiful shrines— that of Joan of Arc in the marketplace at Rouen, where a bad custom wrought one of its greatest crimes.

To return to LePuy, there is another story of interest to Catholics the world over. When Urban II sent the First Crusade on its way, he appointed Adhémar, Bishop of LePuy, to accompany it as his legate. Adhémar died in 1100 under the

Fortified pilgrim church of Les Saintes Maries de la Mer.

Notre Dame de la Garde, Marseilles, the shrine of the sailors.

91

Architectural ornament, twelfth century, LePuy.

walls of Antioch. He is worth our remembrance, however,
for quite a different kind of activity. He was the author of the
beloved prayer, the *Salve Regina*. Few men's words have been
on the lips of more men and women than those of this bishop
who died over eight hundred years ago.

The *Salve Regina* was known in that time as the *Anti-
phona de Podio*, the Antiphon of LePuy. There is a story about
it in the life of St. Bernard. The saint was wakened one night
by voices singing this antiphon. He rose to find what was
happening and, as he approached the chapel, he felt that the
voices had more than an earthly beauty. When he reached the
chapel he saw that the singers were angels and that they were
singing in the presence of our Blessed Lady. It is said that
St. Bernard particularly loved the hymn, and caused it to be
recited with the office in all the Cistercian monasteries. From

(Over) LePuy, Rocks of St. Michael and Notre Dame de France.

House of Joan of Arc, Domrèmy.

these it spread to the general uses of the Church and has now been added at the end of daily Mass.

Also at LePuy are the Church of St. Michael and the Statue of Notre Dame de France. The former dates back to the eleventh century. The latter, erected in 1860, was cast from cannon metal taken by the French at Sebastopol. The two are built on high pinnacles of volcanic rock which stand out abruptly from the plain. The imagination of our Catholic ancestors has always sought to give meaning to high places by adorning them with images or crucifixes or chapels.

Across the face of France are hundreds of spots in which the souls of the Christian generations have found artistic expression of the faith. On these beautiful and often lonely places the spirit has left its impress on the very stones of the earth, as if to say that even nonliving things should, in the words

Cemetery crucifix at Hunawihr, Alsace.

of the Psalms, bless the Lord. The roadside crucifix at Hunawihr in Alsace, the field shrine at Ventrol, the mountain chapels at Conques and Orcival are merely samples of the multitudinous ways in which the shrines of the past or the present stamp this ancient land of the faith.

One of the striking things about these shrines is the way they have sprung up at various times in history. Many of them occupied the central attention of Catholic France or even of Catholic Europe for centuries and then yielded their place. Such was Vézelay. Such was LePuy. They are still loved for

96

(Above) Field shrine in an
olive orchard, Ventrol.

(Above right) The Chapel
of Matisse at Vence, Mari-
time Province, showing St.
Dominique.

Detail of sculpture, Rodez.

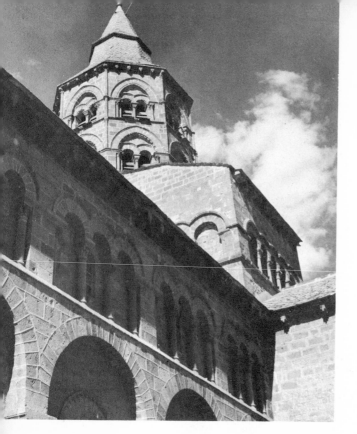

Mountain chapel at Orcival.

their memories, and those who come pray at them. But they no longer attract great pilgrimages, having been replaced in the devotion of Catholics and apparently in the role they play as scenes of the special divine intervention which they once enjoyed.

But this is not to say that devotion itself has dried up. There are powerful spiritual impulses still stirring in France and all over the Catholic world, and these impulses are showing, under different and modern forms, all the vitality of the Middle Ages themselves. Those old times are sometimes called the ages of faith. So they were, in the sense that the faith was not competed with or disputed. But soul for soul our modern time has quite as much faith as had the century of St. Bernard or that of St. Louis. And so there is in our time also a constant reassertion of the old principle in new forms.

Chapel at Conques.

Pilgrimage church at Conques.

*.S. Armed Forces in Eu-
ope, chapel at SHAPE
eadquarters, near Paris.*

Just the other day the papers carried the account of how the last of the high niches in St. Peter's, in which are contained the statues of religious founders, had been filled with the image of St. Louise de Marillac. With the guidance of St. Vincent de Paul, who occupies another niche in St. Peter's, she was the foundress of the Daughters of Charity. We are familiar in the United States with the striking and beautiful costume of these sisters, as different and picturesque as the uniforms of the Swiss Guards themselves. And in France, particularly in Paris, they seem almost to have grown out of the landscape.

The motherhouse of these sisters is in Paris on the rue du Bac. Many people pass up and down this street in the Latin Quarter without ever suspecting what it represents. They see the throngs of students from the Sorbonne and the other phases of the city's life; they come home and talk about these things with more or less understanding. But often they do not penetrate to this other fact of French and Parisian life, this deep spring of religion which brings thousands of dedicated women to spend lives of happy servitude for the welfare of others.

St. Louise lived in the seventeenth century. Ever since that time her community has played a vital role in the Church and is now world-wide in its activities. It has begotten whole generations of holy and beneficent souls and has had its share of saints in the calendar.

One of these was Catherine Labouré, who was chosen in 1830 for the favor of an apparition of our Blessed Lady and who then became her instrument in intensifying the religious life of France and of the world. The very beautiful chapel where the vision appeared, the tomb of the saint, and, most interesting of all, the chair in which our Lady sat while she talked with Catherine can all be visited. Not very far away is the tomb of St. Vincent de Paul, founder both of the Daughters of Charity and of the priests known as Vincentians.

Many will remember the film which presented his life and personality so vividly, *Monsieur Vincent*.

Thus the spirit of religion renews itself from generation to generation. The saints canonized inspire, direct, encourage the saints not canonized and help them to keep at their energetic, patient, and earnest toil in such various works of religion and beneficence as the gathering and distribution of food and clothing to the poor, the work of Catholic education, nursing, visiting the sick. The Sisters of Charity exist in the United States in several independent communities. It is another of the strong channels of influence which originated in France, "the eldest daughter of the Church."

Another current of universal interest which sprang up in France of the seventeenth century is the devotion to the Sacred Heart of our Lord. This originated in the Convent of the Visitation in Paray-le-Monial, a little Burgundian town. St. Margaret Mary Alacoque was a nun in this convent. Here in the chapel our Lord appeared to her frequently and made her the apostle of the devotion to the Sacred Heart. There is, perhaps, no modern form of worship that has spread more widely than this. All over the world Catholics pay special homage to our Saviour on First Fridays because He asked it. His request was made known through this holy woman whose body lies enshrined in the little chapel where she used to hear Him speak. Our picture is not of this chapel but of the great church at Paray-le-Monial. It is a massive structure in Burgundian Romanesque of the twelfth century. It had nothing directly to do with St. Margaret Mary and the apparitions. But the crowds of people who come to the town could never be accommodated in the little convent chapel; therefore the medieval church is the official basilica for the more important ceremonies.

Among the most up-to-date of saints is the one who is honored in the elaborate shrine at Lisieux. The Carmelite nun, whose name in religion was Theresa, is called by her other

Main courtyard and cloister of Sisters of Charity, rue du Bac, Paris.

Sisters of Charity packing supplies for foreign missions.

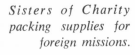

Shrine of St. Vincent de Paul in the chapel, rue du Bac.

Chair of the Apparition, rue du Bac, Paris.

Tomb of St. Catherine Labouré.

*Shrine of St. Theresa
at Lisieux.*

The Church at Paray-le-Monial.

Interior of the Cathedral of St. Peter, Lisieux.

title the Little Flower of Jesus. The fame of this little sister, spreading out of her Norman cloister, has gone through the world like a fragrance of the most penetrating power and has laid its hold literally on millions. They seem to have found in the simple autobiography she left behind some closer approach to the secret of holiness and happiness in God than is conveyed, at any rate to the ordinary seeker, by writers of much greater name and apparently higher authority. Her namesake, St. Theresa of Avila, certainly holds higher place in the eyes of historians and literary people, perhaps even in the eyes of theologians. Yet Theresa of Lisieux is known to every Catholic in the world and is prayed to by many to whom the saint of Avila is little more than a name.

It is not surprising, therefore, to see a most elaborate basilica eclipsing the stern medieval cathedral of the town. Now almost completed, it encloses the relics of this simple person who died when hardly more than a child nearly sixty years ago.

Mont St. Michel.

Of what worldly people want she had very little, and that little she put behind her when she entered the Carmel. But she had the insight of sanctity, which made her spiritual dedication absolute, and that form of genius which is the power to express her thoughts and feelings about God in such a way that the many might catch from her the contagion of holiness. It is to get near to this secret that people go to shrines; therefore, Lisieux has become one of the most famous of all the shrines erected and frequented in our twentieth-century world.

One of the finest experiences possible to a traveler is to come along the Norman coast near Avranches and to see, suddenly appearing across the bay, the monastery of Mont St. Michel. The great Benedictine abbey-fortress buildings rise terrace after terrace up a conical, rocky island to be crowned by the abbey church and by a gilded statue of the archangel Michael. Inspired by a vision of the archangel, Bishop Aubert of Avranches founded the abbey in 708. Existing buildings are of tenth- to fifteenth-century construction.

Normandy's next door neighbor is Brittany, the French province which is renowned for the widespread and fervent practice of religion, and for the way in which the faith colors the outward life of its towns and villages. The Bretons are among the most conservative people in the world. They have been tenacious of their ancient Gaelic tongue, which is in full use as a living language, although French is also spoken everywhere. Their costumes, differing from village to village, do not appear as often as they once did, but they are still worn on feast days in the little Breton churches. In other parts of France local costumes have disappeared altogether.

Brittany possesses none of the major monuments of the Middle Ages. The cathedral of Quimper is probably the most imposing and finest example of Gothic in the province. But there are hundreds of village and small-town churches abounding in the picturesque more than in the beautiful. It is interesting to compare the quaint and humble architecture here

Breton shrine of St. Anne, Auray.   *Child in Breton costume, Finistère.*

Cathedral and ramparts, Quimper.

*Choir boys dressed for the ceremony of
the Pardon of St. Anne.*

with the stateliness and magnificence which characterize Brittany's proud neighbor, Normandy.

The celebrated pardons are the typical religious celebrations of Brittany. These are the special feasts at the more renowned centers to which pilgrimages come from the rest of the province on the appointed days. The name "pardon" is derived from the fact that an indulgence is granted on these days. The various pardons have interesting titles: at Tréguier is celebrated the Pardon of the Poor; at St. Ronan, the Pardon of the Mountain; at St. Anne de le Palude, the Pardon of the Sea. In the coast towns the procession is formed of lines of boats that sail from designated places into the little harbors.

The principal saint of Brittany is St. Anne, and her chief shrine is at Auray on the southern coast of the peninsula. In July there is an impressive pardon here. Those who have received answers to their prayers take part in the procession carrying emblems of the favors granted. All who have witnessed the Breton festivals bear testimony to the fine decorum and spirit of religion with which they are carried out.

We have left to the last the shrine which is the greatest of all in France and, in some senses, the greatest in the world today, the grotto and basilica of Lourdes.

It is almost a hundred years now since the little Bernadette Soubirous knelt at the grotto before the "beautiful lady" who appeared to her. The story is so familiar that it does not need to be retold here except to say that the child made a welcome for her story by candor and consistency and that the Blessed Virgin of the Immaculate Conception made good her command and demonstrated her presence. From the year 1858 to the present, her miraculous intervention has been frequent in the cure of the sick and still more frequent in the conversion of souls to God.

Over 30,000 sick people come to Lourdes each year, bringing suffering in all its dreadful varieties. Great numbers are cured. Today 5,000 doctors have joined an International

Medical Association to study the Lourdes cures. Still greater numbers are not cured. The choice is made by the secret operation of divine Providence; it is not part of God's design that all sorrow should be taken from the world even at Lourdes, even through the intercession of our Lady. But the cures that are granted and that are so palpably miraculous prove the presence of God's mercy and of His Mother's love. This presence is a consolation to those who carry their burdens of pain back with them.

Even more remarkable than the miraculous cures are the spiritual effects on sick and well alike. There is no place where people's souls are more deeply stirred than here, or where faith is more strengthened and confirmed.

The solemn processions at night give special evidence of this. Hundreds of men and women make their way to a statue at the end of the esplanade and then come back to the esplanade in front of the basilica. They carry lighted candles protected by little paper cups. As they stand there massed together their lights resemble a field of glowing flowers. At a given moment the hymns cease and up from the crowd come the words of the Creed, words which are often said casually and conventionally but which now are chanted with the feeling of solemn affirmation, voice accompanying voice and heart speaking to heart. To take part in such an act must necessarily be one of the high moments of any life. It is like taking part in one of the visions of the Apocalypse.

This assertion of the faith in the spiritual is, after all, the purpose for which all Catholic shrines exist. It is spiritually helpful to visit any place where others have found evidence of the divine participation in the affairs of men. Shall we be challenged if we say that of all such places in our modern world Lourdes gives the strongest and most continuous evidence of such intervention from heaven? It is good to know that God and our Lady lighted this bright lamp of the supernatural within the land of France.

Grotto of the Apparition
Lourdes.

Here the sick are brought b
pilgrimage trains, the Whi
Trains. They are cared for b
a band of volunteer attendant
including some former invalid
called the Hospitallers of Ou
Lady of Lourdes, a men'
group organized for this servic
in 1884.

A great procession at Lourdes.

(Right) Lourdes, Chapel of St. Bernadette. (Below) Basilica and esplanade at Lourdes.

f the more than one thousand nnual pilgrimages to Lourdes, ost famous are the mid-August ational Pilgrimage, started in 872, and the early-October osary Pilgrimage, in its forty-xth year in 1954. More than o million visitors come each ar, among them 1500 doctors ho call at the Medical Bureau.

Chapel of the Rosary, Lourdes.

SPAIN

SPAIN, LIKE ITALY, HAD ITS FRONTIERS made by nature. Except on the Portuguese side, Spain is marked out geographically as a unit. Within its borders of mountain and sea it has the specialty of being, after Switzerland, the highest country in Europe, for the greater part of it is on high tableland averaging about two thousand feet above sea level.

The individuality of these physical facts would seem to have much to do with the strikingly individual characteristics of the Spanish people. More than any other nationality, they are said to hold their ancient racial characteristics.

As for all the European countries west of the Adriatic, the history of Spain begins with the Roman conquest. It is true that some fragments of information are available even from Paleolithic times and that some general knowledge has been developed by archaeologists about the inhabitants of the peninsula in the Iron Age. But consecutive knowledge dates

The Alcázar, high above the river Clamores, Segovia.

Roman bridge near Santander

(Opposite) The wall of the
Pyrenees, Torla.

(Below left) Children at village near Villacastin. (Below right) Farmer wearing
wooden shoes on elevated pegs, typical of the northern coast, Santilluna del Mar.

from about three centuries before Christ when the Romans began the series of wars which finally drove Carthage out of Spain and made possible the reduction of the country to the legal and cultural system of the Empire. This Roman hegemony lasted for about six centuries and left Spain with numerous monumental reminders of its greatness in the form of roads, aqueducts, bridges, theaters, circuses, temples, reservoirs, and the like.

The best thing that the Roman Empire did for Spain was that it fulfilled its providential role of providing a theater for the diffusion of Christianity. Saragossa and Compostela are associated in legend with the beginnings of the faith in apostolic times. The story of the Church gradually emerges with its usual accompaniment of martyrdom. The Spanish Christians early learned the art of suffering for their belief. With the advent of peaceful times after the conversion of

Constantine in the fourth century the church of Spain took its full part with the rest of the Christian world in developing the doctrine, the liturgy, the social and cultural life of Christian antiquity. One of the famous popes of the time, St. Damasus, and the Christian poet Prudentius, were from Spain.

This Catholic Christianity stood the test in the rough years of the fifth and sixth centuries when the waves of the barbaric tribes swept over it in the tide that reached to Roman Africa. One after the other came, the Alans, the Vandals, the Suevians, the Visigoths. The last settled for a while in the northeast, which was called for them Gothalandia. Time has softened the name into Catalonia. The Visigoths then spread their domination over their predecessors. Like their contemporaries in Italy, France, and elsewhere, they accepted the religion, and as we have seen, the tongue of the conquered province, although Catholic orthodoxy did not prevail without a century of struggle. The unification of the Visigothic kingdom came about at the close of the sixth century and is associated with St. Hermenegild, who died a martyr's death in the Catholic cause, and Reccared, who sealed the political and religious unity of the kingdom in 589. The court of this regime was at Toledo, which was also the seat of numerous ecclesiastical councils that influenced the Church not only in Spain but throughout the continent.

The contribution of the Visigoths was definite but short-lived. It ended with the defeat of Roderick the Goth in 711 at the hands of the Moslems invading from North Africa. It was the first western onrush of this terrific military thrust which carried its arms as far as central France. In France the invaders were defeated by Charles Martel and driven back across the Pyrenees, but in Spain they remained and took ascendancy over the Christian population. The Arab capital was established at Cordova and its government was so complete as to leave at first vestiges of independence only in the mountains of the north in the little kingdoms of Asturias, Navarre, Aragon,

Franciscan brother near Assisi.

*The Cathedral,
Salamanca, Spain.*

*Tomb of St. James the Apostle
at Santiago de Compostela, Spain*

and Catalonia. Here the remnants of the Christian culture gathered their broken strength and before long started out on the long trial of winning back Spain to independence and unity and Christian culture. The first battle of this "Reconquest" was at Covadonga, where Pelayo beat the invaders in 718. It reached its crisis in the eleventh century with the victories of the Cid and those of Alfonso VI of Castile, who took Toledo from the Moors in 1085. It became decisive with the victory of Alfonso VIII in 1212 at Las Navos de Tolosa. It arrived at its last episode when Ferdinand of Aragon and Isabella of Castile drove out the last of the Moors from Granada in 1492, restored the entire peninsula to unity, and initiated the tradition of "the Catholic Kings."

The struggle for independence, national and religious, thus lasted for more than seven centuries. It is one of the most singular features of European history for the patience, the endurance, the single-mindedness of an entire people.

The sixteenth century opened with an epoch of glory. The Spanish genius dominated most of Europe and most of the new discoveries beyond the seas. Their religious initiative during this period was one of the greatest forces making for the reorganization of Catholic Europe after the great Revolt. They led in theology, in ecclesiastical policy, in the spirit of mysticism, in religious organization. The Church owes to them the Society of Jesus, the Spiritual Exercises of St. Ignatius, the mystical treatises of Theresa of Avila and John of the Cross, the theological treatises of Suarez, the foundations of international law with Vittoria.

Time came for the decay of the Spanish Empire and of the Spanish predominance. The last few centuries have seen the retirement of Spanish political power to its own territory. But its people and their tongue have taken over the southern continent of America and the foundations have been laid for destinies which will, please God, be glorious.

Toledo, the medieval capital of Spain, represents her

history much better than Madrid, the present capital, which is a "made" city dating only from the seventeenth century. The cathedral was begun by Ferdinand the Saint in 1227 just as Christian Spain was beginning to feel secure in its independence. The building was continued through many generations. It is Gothic, but in the Spanish tradition. It is the second largest church in Spain, and one of the four or five largest in the world, and it abounds in every variety of artistic treasure.

The town is rich in other churches, in which some of the principal works of El Greco, Velasquez, and others are preserved. Lastly its Alcazar will long be remembered for its siege in the Civil War of 1936 to 1939.

Far in the northwestern hills of Spain is the town of Covadonga with the grotto where Pelayo and his followers at first took refuge, and the basilica of our Lady where Spaniards still thank heaven for past favors and ask it for new ones. The church is a recent one, having been built in 1874 to replace the old one which had been destroyed by fire in 1777. It is not among the leading monuments architecturally, but it stands on an impressive hill and it is very venerable, even among the shrines of Spain, for its commemoration of seven centuries of courage.

Far out in the northwest province of Galicia, close to the Atlantic, is Spain's most famous shrine, that of St. James of Compostela. St. James the Greater, brother of John and privileged with him and Peter to be a witness of the Transfiguration and of the Agony in the Garden, was put to death in Jerusalem in the year 44. According to Spanish tradition, however, he is thought to have exercised a short apostolate in Spain. It is further believed that his relics were brought back to the country of his predilection and that they were enshrined here close to the sea. The veneration of this shrine dates back to the tenth century. The following century saw it reach the height of celebrity and thereafter, throughout the Middle Ages, the place was, after Rome and Jerusalem, the pilgrimage center

…trance to the Escorial. The monastery of …n Lorenzo el Escorial was founded in …63 by Philip II to commemorate the vic-…ry of San Quentin (1557) and was named … the martyred St. Laurence because the …ttle was won on his day. Formerly used as …onastery, church, and royal palace, it is now a museum.

Young farmer in Central Spain with typical black oxen.

…etail of entrance to the cathedral at Toledo.

par excellence of all Europe. As its fame grew its custodians sought to enhance the splendor of the surroundings. The existing cathedral was begun in the Romanesque of the twelfth century; in succeeding generations the Gothic and Renaissance styles succeeded. The Baroque development of the latter style, of which we saw much in Italy, achieved a fabulous development in Spain, where it is known as Churriguerresque from its principal practitioner, Churriguerra. This style is magnificently exhibited in the façade of Sant Iago, which displays an architectural restlessness and complication brought into unity by an artistic control that is truly wonderful. It takes us a step beyond some of the Italian Baroque and has a grandeur and dignity for all its decoration that is comparable with the Gothic itself.

Another example of Spanish Baroque, or Churriguer-

The church of Covadonga seen from the caves in which the miraculous image was found by Pelayo.

Our Lady of Covadonga
at feast time.

(Left) Façade of the church of Santiago de Compostela, dedicated to James the Apostle. (Below) Closeup of pillar, showing James smiling. (Opposite) Interior and high altar.

resque, is found at the next most celebrated shrine, the Church of Our Lady of the Pillar at Saragossa. This city (whose name derives from Caesar Augustus) was the chief city of Aragon and had traditions connected with the story of St. James. The veneration of the statue of the Blessed Virgin of the Pillar is very widespread among Spaniards, and it is not surprising to find here a most elaborate church, remarkable for its many cupolas with their roofs of colored tiles. The effect, however, is not so unified as that given by the façade at Compostela.

Cathedral at Saragossa, which houses the shrine of Our Lady of Pilar.

Cathedral at Valladolid.   *Oldest part of cathedral at Salamanca.*

Main door to cathedral at Salamanca.

Simpler and more effective is the cathedral of Salamanca. Its two domes lend stature and grandeur to the long straight roof ridge and blend into a picture that is clearly one. Its site over the river Tormes is wonderfully duplicated in the reflections on the water, although the effect is somewhat spoiled by the inharmonious buildings which occupy the slope of the hill between church and river. The church façades are marvels of late Gothic richness, the Spanish taste for the elaborate coming out at its best here.

Interestingly enough, Salamanca was one of the places of refuge during the penal days in the British Isles. The Irish College of Salamanca instituted in those times closed in 1953. The city was also the seat of the most famous of the Spanish universities, which in the Middle Ages ranked with Oxford, Paris, and Bologna. Later, great contributions were made to theology by the doctors whose volumes are known under the name of *Salamanticenses*.

Valladolid was the capital of the old kingdom of Castile. In 1469 Queen Isabella was married here to King Ferdinand. This wedding, which brought about the union of Spain,

Cathedral at Avila, begun in the late twelfth century, completed in the fifteenth.

St. Theresa, Avila.

The fortified wall at Avila.

presaged the decline of Valladolid's prominence, and in 1560 Philip II made Madrid the capital of the united kingdom. However, Valladolid remained a cathedral town and was sufficiently important to build a new cathedral in the sixteenth century. The front of the church shown here is an interesting contrast to many of the other churches we have seen, being, for Spain, relatively simple and restrained, influenced greatly by the prestige of the ancient classical styles. The chief artistic interest of the cathedral is a magnificent silver tabernacle made in 1590, one of the most famous treasures in the country. Another remarkable church in Valladolid is that of San Pablo,

The cathedral at Burgos.

connected with the Dominican convent, a Gothic structure
whose façade is adorned in the rich style known as Plateresque.
This style, characteristic of the Renaissance period before the
onset of the Baroque, gets its name from *plata* (silver plate).
The ornamental parts of the architectural surfaces were treated
in such a way as to suggest the work of silversmiths. Not as
exciting a style as the Churriguerresque, which came after, it
is exquisitely original. Nothing in Spain is more Spanish than
the churches and buildings adorned in this way.

Avila of the Knights is famous as a town with atmosphere.
Its old walled fortifications are among the best preserved in
Europe.

Avila is best known today for its most famous citizen,

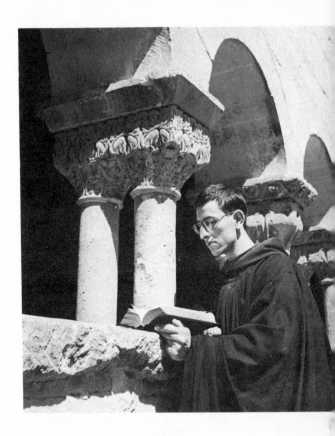

*(Above) The cloister in the monastery of
Santo Domingo de Silos. (Top right) Benedictine friar at Silos.*

The cathedral at Segovia.

*Side tower of the Church
of San Isidoro, León.*

The Church of San Isidoro, León.

Tombs of "the Catholic Kings," Ferdinand and Isabella, Granada.

vish baroque design
the Carthusian monas-
ry, Granada. A ceiling
om the same monastery
shown on the end-
papers of this book.

who is also one of the most famous Spaniards, St. Theresa. This remarkable woman, who lived between 1515 and 1582, had the strange combination of qualities which we noted in St. Bernard and others: she was an administrator and foundress, very active in what might be called the business side of the religious life; at the same time she was a contemplative and mystic. One of those gifted with the power to reach out into the supernatural in vision and ecstasy. she had also the mission to communicate her mystical experience in writings which have remained classics of theology and literature. The poet Crashaw spoke of her as having the qualities of the eagle and the dove. This may serve to put in one phrase the forceful paradox of one of the greatest of the saints. The convent of St. Theresa occupies the site of her birthplace.

The city of Burgos presents us with a cathedral which is probably more akin to the Gothic of France than any other of the peninsular churches. It was begun in 1221 and was continued in the usual way over a period of about three centuries. Its side walls are very rich in Plateresque ornamentation.

The cathedral contains the tomb of El Cid Campeador (the Lord Champion). This celebrated man took a leading part in the eleventh-century struggle which turned the tide of war against the Moorish power. His individual exploits were so exceptional as to make him a hero of romance, and the chief medieval Spanish epic builds around the historic figure a wealth of legend in which he becomes the symbol of the whole Reconquest, the Spanish analogue of the French Roland or the English King Arthur.

Near Burgos is the monastery of Silos. This foundation goes back to the sixth century and is one of the oldest in Spain. It is called after St. Dominic, who was its second founder in the eleventh century and who must not be confused with the later and more renowned St. Dominic, founder of the Order of Preachers. The beautiful cloister of San Domingo de Silos

*Pilgrimage to the ruins of Clonmacnois, Ireland,
on the annual feast of St. Ciaran, September 9.*

The ruins of Greyabbey in County Down, Northern Ireland,
an important Cistercian monastery founded in 1193, which
shows a marked early English influence in style.

is now occupied by Benedictines who have made it a liturgical center and who are among the principal custodians in Spain of the best tradition of Gregorian chant.

Segovia, which holds so many memories of the Roman epoch, has an especially fine example of Gothic architecture in its cathedral front and in the Alcazar, which is magnificently situated 262 feet above the river Clamores. These give some slight impression of Segovia, one of the richest towns in artistic and historic treasures.

León derives its name from the Roman legion which had its headquarters here. In the early days of the Reconquest the city became the capital of one of the oldest independent states. This kingdom of León was afterward united with Castile, and Isabella, who was queen of both kingdoms, brought them into union with Aragon by her marriage to Ferdinand. In León is one of the most important monuments of the Romanesque period—the Church of San Isidoro. It is the burial place of a large number of the kings and queens of the Middle Ages who led in the struggle for the assertion of Spanish and Christian independence. The cathedral is a splendid example of very early Gothic.

Southern Spain presents us with two of her most celebrated cities: Granada and Seville. Granada is best known perhaps for its Moorish buildings, the Alhambra and the Genaralife. The Moorish style is understandable inasmuch as this southern part of the country was the first to fall under the Moslems and the last to be taken from them. While cities to the north had been in Christian hands for centuries, Granada still remained Moorish, although the basic element of the population itself was Christian. But as always happens in these circumstances it was a population under persecution; therefore, the Christian monuments of Granada date from the period after its liberation by Ferdinand and Isabella. Its cathedral is of the sixteenth century, in a Gothic similar to that of

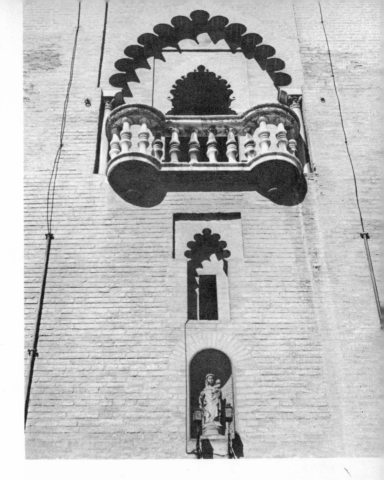

(Right) Detail of the Giralda, the bell tower of the cathedral of Seville.

(Right) The cathedral at Seville.

(Left) Gate at Seville.

*The casket of Columbus car-
ried by four knights, Seville.*

Toledo. It contains the splendid tombs of Ferdinand and
Isabella. Another remarkable church is that of the Carthusian
monastery, north of the city, which was built as a memorial
to the "Great Captain," Gonzalo de Córdoba, who died in
1515. Built during the Baroque period, this church exhibits
to what excess the lavishness of the Baroque might go.

The other southern city, probably the most admired in
Spain, is Seville. This part of the south was taken away from
Moorish control in the thirteenth century by Ferdinand III.
Its cathedral, therefore, dates from the late Gothic period and
is, after St. Peter's, the largest church in the world. It has

Monastery of La Rabida, where Columbus stayed before his voyage to America.

Church at Palos de la Frontera, where Columbus heard his last mass before departure for the New World.

also one of the richest interiors: its painting and sculpture are representative of every country in Europe and to cover their subject matter would be to review the whole history of Spain and of the Church. The most celebrated feature of the cathedral is its bell tower. It is called the Giralda (the weather vane) from the revolving figure at its summit, a statue of faith placed there in 1568. The tower itself was originally the minaret of a mosque built before the Christians took the city.

The cathedral also contains the tomb of Columbus. The discoverer's remains were first buried in Seville. They were transferred to Santo Domingo in about 1540. When that island passed under French control they were carried to

Havana. At the outbreak of the Spanish-American War they were brought back to Seville to be honored in this magnificent monument. It is a spot that means much to everyone who understands something of history and is especially dear to Americans who are the beneficiaries of the great discoverer.

We may also find interesting the gateway of the convent of La Rabida where Friar Juan Perez was superior when Columbus knocked at the gate in an hour of dejection. The church of Palos is also of importance here, for it was from this port in 1492 that the three little ships set out which were to change the future of the world.

The monastery at Guadalupe, almost as rich as Seville Cathedral in artistic and historical treasure, is reminiscent of the mixture of Moorish and Christian culture in the Middle Ages. The striking cloister is in the style known as

Monastery of Guadalupe, founded by Alfonso XI in 1340 to commemorate his victory over the Moors at Salado.

The Virgin of Guadalupe with flower offerings of pilgrims.

bove right) Portals of the church of Guadalupe.
bove) The Mudejar cloister and temple at Guadalupe.
ght) Detail of the monastery gate, Guadalupe.

Mudejar, so called from the name given to Moslems who were subjects of the Christian kingdoms, just as the name of Mozarabs belonged to Christians living under the Moors. The church and cloisters represent a struggle of different styles and periods—Moorish, Gothic, and Renaissance. The monastery, housing the Hieronymite friars, was one of the richest and most influential in Spain. It had a renowned library and was a center of scientific studies, particularly in medicine. But all this learning never succeeded in bringing unity to the buildings, which are a collection of magnificent fragments and a kind of museum of Spanish architectural history. The celebrated Virgin of Guadalupe, a statue of unknown origin, shares with the Pilar of Saragossa and the monastery of Montserrat the veneration of Spaniards for our Lady.

Montserrat, monastic buildings.

Placed high in difficult mountain terrain, the shrine at Montserrat is interesting for its antiquity and for the fact that it has been so long held in reverence, rather than for any outstanding architectural quality or beauty of decoration. The name has a romantic sound to those who recall the legends of the Middle Ages. Music lovers will recall the song of Lohengrin "In Fernem Land" in which the knight reveals to Elsa that the Holy Grail rested in Monsalvat (Montserrat) in a temple so rich and precious that nothing on earth could be compared to it. Such was the dream. The reality is a place magnificent for the mountain solitudes rather than for man's handiwork. In such places as Montserrat the soul can find moments of aspiration and of close association with the heavenly.

The shrine of Loyola, built around the birthplace of St. Ignatius, is undoubtedly one of the most important shrines in this chapter. This saint has a high place in two calendars of

Montserrat, the entrance to the church.

141

Main building at Loyola, the birthplace of St. Ignatius.

(Below right) One of the chapels at Loyola. (Below left) Loyola, main entrance.

greatness, that of Spain and that of the universal Church. Few greater things exist in the annals of Christendom than the exploits of the society which he founded to oppose the tides of revolt which swept over the Church in the sixteenth century. In that century, to use Macaulay's words, "the Church of Rome, having lost a large part of Europe, not only ceased to lose, but actually regained nearly half of what she had lost." In this achievement there were many factors, and a good many of them came from Spain. There was certainly no factor more

Life-sized sculpture of St. Ignatius carved by Valera in cedar wood with gold and color added.

important than the advance of the Jesuits to the defense. The greatest schoolmasters, theologians, missionaries, diplomats, administrators, tacticians, seemed to be in endless supply from the society which had been initiated by the inspiration of this marvelous man.

The reader will remember how Ignatius, son of a noble family, began life as a soldier in the wars against the French. While recovering from a wound at Loyola his mind became occupied with thoughts of religion and finally he was privileged with a vision of the Blessed Virgin with the Child. This event marked his complete conversion from whatever worldliness he had been given to previously. He began a long and rigorous training in personal devotion and asceticism, and a further training in Paris in theology and other studies necessary to his growing purpose, which was to dedicate his life and to direct other lives to the service of the Church in an age of crisis. His first six companions took vows with him in Paris. They then went to Rome where their work, after some trial and testing, was approved and where Ignatius spent the rest of his life directing his soldier-followers in the spiritual warfare which they fought so brilliantly.

The statue of St. Ignatius shown here is placed near the site of the room in which his conversion took place. It is a statue marked by the characteristic Spanish quality of intensity and conveys most dramatically the power and strength of that historic moment.

The gifts of Spain began far back in the days when she was the bastion of Christendom against the armed assault of Islam. They continued through the time when she laid the foundations of civilization in our Western Hemisphere, and were increased by her services to the unity of the Church in the worst crisis of her history, that of the sixteenth century. In our time the service of Spain has been renewed by her leadership in keeping the Iron Curtain from descending over western Europe.

PORTUGAL

THOUGH PORTUGAL OCCUPIES BUT A SMALL part of the European continent and, for that matter, but a small part of the Iberian peninsula, it nevertheless has played a large role in history. And in our own time it plays a large one in the devotional life of the Church by reason of the marvels of Fatima.

The extraordinary intervention of heaven in the affairs of men has taken different forms at different times. In recent centuries it has been most often in the form of the apparition of our Blessed Lady to children. This has happened more than once in France, notably at La Salette and at Lourdes. The most striking events of the kind since Lourdes in 1858 have been the visions of Fatima in 1917. On five occasions, in consecutive months from May to September, the Blessed Virgin showed herself to the shepherd children in this lonesome, unheard-of spot of the earth. She told them of the things she wanted to communicate to them and to the world:

Pilgrims doing penance at the shrine of Our Lady of Fatima.

the need of constant prayer, the value of suffering, the punishment of sins, certain features of the future of the world. Very strangely, for that year 1917, in the third apparition she spoke of the danger that Russia was to bring to the world and of the need for that country's conversion. She said that through Russia great errors would be spread in the world, issuing in war and persecution for the Church. But she promised that in the end Russia would be converted, and consecrated by the Holy Father to her Immaculate Heart, and that peace would be given to mankind. In the last of the five apparitions to the children she said she would grant cures to the sick, "but not to all."

During the apparitions, the Blessed Virgin announced that a great miracle would be wrought in October. The news of the message awakened some belief and some skepticism, but in any case great interest. On the morning of October 13, 1917, enormous crowds gathered at Fatima to witness the miracle, or to scoff if it were not realized. The children had their vision as before. Our Lady told them that the people should repent of their sins and ask God's pardon. Then she disappeared. As she did so, the strange miracle of the sun occurred. The great globe changed its color, appeared to spin on its axis and to approach the earth. Then suddenly it stopped, receded, and took its customary place.

This marvelous event was witnessed by thousands of people who had come to see it, many of whom are still alive. Since the possibility of the miracle had been announced at large, it was attended also by representatives of the press and was described in the Portuguese newspapers of the time just as any other extraordinary event might be. At first it was unknown outside Portugal, but gradually the word of it spread. It has resulted in huge pilgrimages to this formerly humble and unknown village.

In 1928 a basilica was begun. In 1931 it was the scene of the solemn dedication of Portugal to God and to our Lady; 300,000 persons came to take part in the procession and to accept this dedication pronounced by the Papal Nuncio and by the Cardinal Patriarch of Lisbon. Every year the attendance has increased and the devotion of the rosary, of the nocturnal adoration, and the like have grown in fervor. The miracles of healing, like those at Lourdes, have been beyond number. Those officially listed by the medical bureau established for the purpose of investigating the cures already are numbered in the hundreds. Many others, not officially admitted, are being added.

Since World War I, and still more since the second, an immense growth has taken place in the pilgrimage movement of Catholics from all free parts of the world. In this, there is nothing more striking than the increase in the crowds that go to Fatima. At all times of the year, but converging especially on October 13, which is the anniversary of the great public apparition, the numbers of the devout are now enormous.

Here then, as at Lourdes, the divine mercy and forgiveness are shown in striking forms. As in the case of the miracles of our Lord Himself, these special signs and wonders are done with a purpose over and above the mere granting of favors. The purpose is that the faith of the millions should be intensified where it exists or restored where it has been lost. The real good of these wonderful places is not the granting of temporal favors but the increase of the spiritual life.

There is a particular accent in the devotions at Fatima. Spirituality of life is connected with the problem of the world's peace as cause to effect. That was the message of the Blessed Virgin to the world through the children of Fatima. That is the message which the Church inculcates at the shrine and in the Fatima devotions held throughout the world. The disasters of the wars of this century, hot and cold, are due to many causes. The chief of these is in the spiritual realm. A materialistic outlook on life destroys the spirit of man. It also destroys peace. A spiritual outlook, influencing citizens in their masses and multitudes, is an absolute requisite for stabilizing society, for nullifying the clamor of demagogues, for sanctioning tranquillity, and for banishing war. It is this spirit, glimpsed in the wonderful picture of the Portuguese pilgrims, which it is the destiny of Fatima to increase. The first purpose of this, as of all Catholic shrines, is to sanctify the individual souls of men and bring them to heaven. But at Fatima, as everywhere, a blessing goes forth to all the world in the intensification of the consciousness of the spiritual which is the irreducible and indispensable element of good citizenship and peace.

Crowds attend ceremonies at basilica of Our Lady of Fatima.

Typical crowd and visiting archbishop.

The statue of Our Lady of Fatima.

GERMANY

THE PATHWAYS OF THE HERALDS OF THE
gospel, which at first proceeded westward
and northwestward, finally reached the ends of the European
world and then turned back toward Eastern Europe. In the
seventh century and later, St. Columbanus and the Irish pil-
grim-monks established the faith in places where it had not
existed and intensified it in places where it had been weak.
Meanwhile Northern and Central Europe was still in the dark-
ness of paganism.

The great name associated with the introduction of the
faith in this region is that of the Englishman, St. Boniface. For
his mission of converting the heathen lands, he received the
authorization of Pope Gregory II, who consecrated him Bishop
of Germany and of all the lands east of the Rhine. He gave
thirty-five years of his life to his mission and was put to a
martyr's death by heathens in the Netherlands, but he left
behind him a settled Church in lands which were to yield to

*King Solomon, detail of altarpiece by Heinrich Douwermann in the fifteenth-century
church of St. Nicholas at Kalkar. (Above) The Kiedrich Madonna (1330).*

151

The Cathedral at Fulda, built 1704–1712, contains the crypt of St. Boniface. (Left) The altar with the silver treasures of the Cathedral.

none in the depth and splendor of their Christian culture, lands which for the most part are still among the fairest regions of the faith.

Through the centuries St. Boniface's relics have been venerated at Fulda, which consequently has been held in great honor as the center of German Catholicism. Here in the great baroque cathedral the bishops of Germany begin their annual meetings with prayer for guidance in one of the most difficult periods which the Church has known. In 1954 they celebrated the twelfth centenary of the death of St. Boniface. The occasion gave them and us good cause to remember the centuries of trial the Church has come through and to have confidence that God's providence will bring it through the storms of the present age.

Germany is full of monuments that recall the dawn of medieval civilization. The church at Hildesheim is of the eleventh century. It replaced the first shrine raised to our

Blessed Lady in the lands then newly converted by St. Boniface. The original church was donated by the Emperor Louis the Pious, and was second to none in the veneration it received through the Middle Ages. In the eleventh century when the arts of building and sculpture burgeoned all over Europe, Hildesheim was among the leaders under its great abbot St. Bernward. Its bronze doors representing Biblical scenes belong to that dawn of beauty. The splendid church was damaged in the last war, but its chief treasures have been preserved.

The Cathedral of Cologne is one of the outstanding examples of Gothic architecture in all of Europe, and its presence dominates the whole of the city. Built between 1248 and the end of the sixteenth century, its impressive towered front was not actually completed until the latter part of the nineteenth century. It contains many famous works of art, including the shrine of the Three Magi, the treasury with the shrines of St. Maurinus and St. Albinus, and the shrines of St. Heribert and St. Engelbert. It suffered severe damage in the last war.

The German artistic genius was characterized by a love of richness. Examples of this in the medieval period are the coronation reredos at Bad Oberdorf and the altar of the Seven Sorrows at Kalkar. A note of tender playfulness is found in the Kiedrich Madonna and in the St. Elizabeth at Marburg.

The Cathedral in Cologne, largest of all German churches and one of the chief monuments of Gothic architecture in Europe.

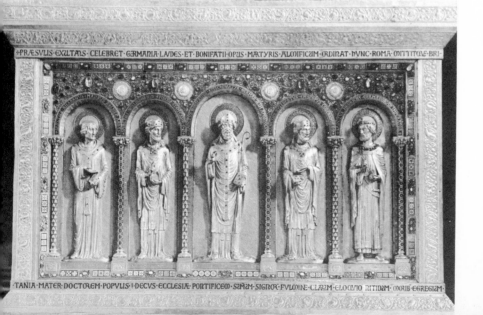

+ PRÆSVLIS · EXVLTANS · CELEBRET · GERMANIA · LAVDES · ET · BONIFATII · OPVS · MÆTYRIS · ALQNIFICVM · ORDINAT · HVNC · ROMA · QITTITQVE · BRI-

TANIA · MATER · DOCTOREM · POPVLIS · I · DECVS · ECCLESIÆ · PONTIFICEQ · SVNVM · SIGNOR · FVLQINE · CLARVM · ELOQVIO · NITIDVM · QORIB · EGREGIVM ·

(Above) Reredos of the Coronation at Bad Oberdorf.
(Right) Head of St. Bartholomew, part of the fifteenth-
century carved "Altar of the Virgin" in the Church of Our
Lord at Creglingen.

(Opposite) Two of the famed, eleventh-century door
reliefs in the Cathedral at Hildesheim, depicting the
history of mankind from the creation to its salvation by
Christ. (Bottom opposite) The altar of St. Boniface in
the Benedictine abbey of Maria Laach in the Eifel.

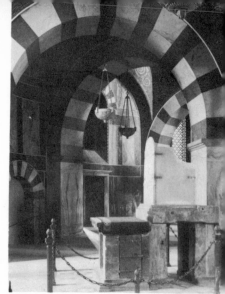

Fine Gothic sculpture by Adam Krafft (1493–1496) in St. Lawrence Church in Nuremberg.

On the other hand, we see feeling for dignity and strength in the noble head of St. Bartholomew at Creglingen. The same spirit survives in modern work such as the Altar of St. Boniface at Maria Laach.

The curious accumulation of architectural styles in the Cathedral of Aachen reflects its long and complicated history.

(Above) The Cathedral of St. Martin at Mainz, founded in the eleventh century. (Left) The seven-towered Cathedral of St. George, on the river Lahn at Limburg.

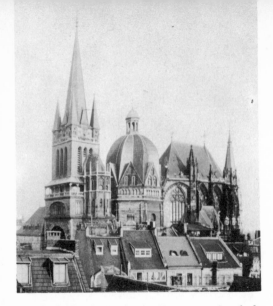

The Cathedral of Aachen, Germany. Its holy relics are the focal point of the Aachen Pilgrimage each July. (Left) In a niche in the uppermost story stands Charlemagne's throne.

(Right) St. Peter's Cathedral at Worms, a twelfth-century building in the purest Romanesque style in Germany.

Here again we are brought to the dawn, or even predawn, of medieval art in portions of the church which go back to the days when Charlemagne held his court here and for a while gave substance to the elusive dream of European unity. That dream was half secular and half spiritual, and it retained such marvellous fascination for the medieval mind that Charlemagne was often regarded as a saint and his tomb was looked upon with religious veneration. The cathedral grew in dimensions and in the wealth of relics and art treasures. The lovely choir with its stained glass has something of the character of St. Louis's Sainte Chapelle in Paris.

The noble simplicity and strength of the Romanesque period can be seen in the "Emperors' Cathedrals" of Mainz and Worms. To this inherent strength of architectural styling the Cathedral of Limburg adds its imposing position. In upper Bavaria stands the early Romanesque "Holy Chapel" of Altotting. Built in the seventh century, it contains a miraculous sacred image. Together with the parish and pilgrimage church built in the thirteenth to fifteenth centuries, it constitutes a famous pilgrimage center of the Holy Virgin. Germany has a multitude of magnificent and deservedly admired Gothic monuments, but there is something about the Romanesque that brings the venerable and the human into a very special blending. No country has excelled, or perhaps even equaled, Germany in this.

After the Middle Ages and the religious revolt of the sixteenth century there came a striking reassertion of Catholic life in the various countries of Europe, which often goes by the misnomer of Counter Reformation. This movement was nowhere more vigorous than in the German lands. Among its most striking manifestations was the originality and power of its architecture. Renaissance had by this time developed into baroque. The German churchmen and architects, still inspired

Two masterpieces of eighteenth-century baroque. (Left) Pilgrimage church of the Fourteen Saints, "Vierzehnheiligen," in Upper Franconia near Bamberg. (Right) Fürstenfeldbrück in Upper Bavaria. The interior of this Cistercian church is the work of Fr. Appiani.

(Left) The Benedictine monastery of Zweifalten in Württemberg. (Right) The pilgrimage church of Weiskirche in Upper Bavaria, dedicated to the "Scourging of Our Lord."

by the medieval taste for richness, gave baroque style manifold expression in the churches and monasteries of the seventeenth and eighteenth centuries. The Church of the Fourteen Holy Martyrs shows the conservative side of baroque. The interior of Fürstenfeldbrück gives you the style in its more exciting and, perhaps, more frequent mood. The pulpit at Zweifalten shows the style at its apogee, or perhaps slightly past it. In Upper Bavaria is the famous Wieskirche, a pilgrimage church dedicated to the "Scourging of Our Lord." Perhaps the finest rococo church in Germany, it was built in 1746–1754 by Dominikus Zimmerman. The baroque was particularly susceptible of exaggeration, but at its best it can give a very noble expression of religious feeling. And Germany contains a wealth of examples of baroque at its best.

A period not too far behind us was a very tragic one for

(*Above*) *Beirbach. Procession of the Blessed Sa*
rament. (*Left*) *A wayside crucifix in Bavaria.*

(*Below*) *The Benedictine Monastery at Etta*
Bavaria, with the famous pilgrimage church of th
Holy Virgin, founded in 1330, rebuilt in th
eighteenth century.

*Scenes from the Passion
Play at Oberammergau,
1950. First put on by the
people of this Bavarian
village in 1634, it will
be repeated in 1960. It
commemorates the escape
of the village from the
plague. The scenes show
Alois Lang, who recited
the prologue; Christ
with the Apostles; the
Descent from the Cross;
and Mary and Christ.*

Germany and the rest of the world. But the great crimes of history are always the result of movements which take people away from their faith and religious loyalty. When such movements subside, we can see again the things that make life beautiful for decent and honorable people of any land. The wayside crucifix still means much to the Bavarian farmer and to the understanding traveller. And the processions of great feasts, carried out with the German feeling for good order and reverence, still keep alive the Germany which had such strong appeal to Americans of past generations and which gave so much to the formative years of our own culture. The spirit of Oberammergau has done much for the life of the spirit of all modern peoples, and promises much in providing bonds of friendship and peace.

AUSTRIA AND
SWITZERLAND

THE SPLENDID CHURCH ARCHITECTURE OF
Germany, particularly in the south, and the
prevalence of wayside shrines give an effect of what might be
called high visibility to religion. This effect is likewise characteristic of Austria and of the more Catholic parts of Switzerland.

One of the most spectacular religious buildings in the
world is the Abbey of Melk. As an institution, this foundation
dates from the twelfth century, but the buildings are of the
eighteenth century. Here the baroque is at its most dignified
and best. The long line of the massive monastery terminates
in a noble dome flanked by two great towers. This structure
occupies a hill dominating the river and highroad in a most
striking way. The location, besides being physically impressive,
is rich in historical associations, which begin at the time when
the Roman legions used it as a lookout. Warriors of the Middle
Ages built their castles here, and when they gave the site over

*Heiligenkreuz, the oldest Cistercian Abbey in Austria,
founded 1135. (Above) Baroque-style chalice.*

163

Pilgrimage cathedral of Gurk, built 1140–1200. [Its]
treasures include a painted Lenten veil by Konrad [von]
Friesach, a high altar carved by Michael Hoenel, a[nd]
a famous lead Pietà by Raphael Donner.

(Top and center left) The Benedictine Abbey on th[e]
Wachau at Melk, the largest abbey in Lower Austri[a.]
It is famed for its library, among the treasures of whic[h]
are two Gutenberg Bibles; for its vineyards; and for i[ts]
baroque architecture. In the crypt the remains of th[e]
Irish St. Coloman are buried.

(Bottom left) The Cistercian abbey of Lilenfeld, settle[d]
in 1206 by monks from Heiligenkreuz. Its buildings i[n]
clude the Abbey Church of the Assumption (1230), [a]
late Romanesque basilica; a Gothic baptistry; a Roman[-]
esque cloister with stained glass from the fourteent[h]
century; and a library of 27,000 volumes.

(Opposite left) Ancient Benedictine abbey of Gottweig[,]
founded 1072, rebuilt after fire in 1718. (Opposite right[)]
Library of the Benedictine abbey of Altenburg.

The Augustinian abbey buildings of Klosterneuberg, outside Vienna. Visitors may see its handsome baroque interior and Romanesque cloister.

to the Benedictines, the new tenants in turn had a fortified monastery. This gave place in more peaceful times to this monument of religion and of culture.

Among the numerous examples of monastic or cathedral groupings which dominate these landscapes in a similar way are the Cistercian Abbey of Lilienfeld and the Cathedral of Gurk. Both of these occupy the heads of high Alpine valleys lending a powerful significance, as of dedication, to the whole

Michael Pacher altar in the pilgrimage church of St. Wolfgang.

Side altar in the parish church of Maria Saal.

countryside. The Benedictine Monastery of Gottweig is another crown of glory on a hilltop. Klosterneuburg is a magnificent grouping which, on the other hand, dominates a wide plain. No country is richer in instances of blending architectural splendor with happy choice of site.

The interiors of these churches and monasteries correspond in magnificence with the exteriors. The libraries of the Benedictine monasteries of Melk and Altenburg give an idea of the wide spectrum of styles of decoration embraced in one period. The altar of All Souls in the parish church of Mondsee is another instance. Here the baroque adornment was applied with a heavy hand. In contrast the Holy Cross Monastery brings us back to more austere concepts of Gothic beauty.

Wood carving with color and gilding is one of the resplendent forms of beauty with which this region is filled. The scene, which was so beloved by these artists, of the Coronation of the Virgin is here given in three different concepts. All these are from parish churches at Maria Saal, St. Wolfgang, and Mauer.

The treasures of gold and other metal work in these Austrian churches are fabulous. Examples are shown here from the eighth and twelfth centuries and from a later period which favored massive adornment.

(opposite) Side altar the parish church Mauer, near Melk.

de altar by Meinrad ggenbichler in the parchurch of Mondsee.

Twelfth-century chalice.

The Cathedral of St. Gall, Switzerland, and (right) its choir stalls carved with scenes from the life of St. Benedict.

Switzerland, from Lucerne eastward and southward, is prevailingly Catholic and of much the same regional character as Austria and Bavaria.

One of the most interesting places in the world for the reader of church history is the town and monastery of St. Gall. The place takes its name from one of the Irish saints who in the time of St. Columbanus did so much to spread the faith and introduce civilized customs into these regions of wild mountains and forests and wilder men. In course of time a monastery grew up, which in the eighth and ninth centuries became the most renowned school in the whole of Europe. Here was built the library which in those famished days was envied as the greatest outside Rome itself. At the time when European learning and culture were in their darkest days of trial, this was a lighthouse and a fortress. The abbey church of the eighteenth century is beautifully designed without and richly

(Left) Pilgrimage church at Einsiedeln. (Right) A mystery play before its doors.

*library of St. Gall.
*pers protect ancient
* beautiful floors.*

furnished within. The library entrance carries a Greek inscription calling it "Temple of the Mind." The town of St. Gall, beautifully situated on the shore of Lake Constance, is still important in ecclesiastical art as the center from which come the most beautiful church vestments now being made.

Einsiedeln is the best known of the Catholic shrines of Switzerland. It is also of ancient origin and the abbey was associated with the colonization and civilization of what was once only a mountain wilderness. A Madonna of ancient origin has long been the object of great devotion and of pilgrimage. Here again the well-ordered life of Germanic Catholic communities gives effect to all forms of religious and cultural activities, such as the medieval mystery plays which are still enacted in the square before the abbey church.

Switzerland also shows its close proximity to France and Italy. At Locarno, the Madonna del Sasso on the hill above the little city speaks of a land and culture with specifically different charms from those of great Alpine heights and valleys.

Choir stalls, Einsiedeln.   *Pilgrimage chapel of Madonna del Sasso, overlooking Locarno.*

THE LOW
COUNTRIES

THE NETHERLANDS, BELGIUM, AND LUXEM-
bourg are small in area but rich in the social
organization of the faith and in the monumental evidences of
Catholic culture. For centuries the people of these countries
have been among the leaders of the Catholic world in every
form of strong outward expression of deeply cherished religious
spirit. In the various methods peculiar to our times, such as the
use of the press or the application of Christian principles in
the organization of labor, these "Benelux" Catholics are highly
successful. But they have not forgotten the traditional values
established through the centuries, and they continue both to
cherish their ancient shrines and to contribute new ones to the
culture of today.

Few people, even among Catholics, think of the Netherlands in terms of a Catholic culture. But the population is more
than 30 per cent Catholic, and this large minority is one
of the strongest and most loyal Catholic groups in devotion to

Procession of penitents at Furnes, Belgium. (Above) A wayside
Pietà in Luxembourg.

the faith and in manifold social expressions of this devotion.

One of the most interesting expressions of this fact is the contribution made by the Dutch Catholics to what is known as contemporary architecture. This style called contemporary has made great advances in every country since World War I though it has met with some resistance in Church circles, which are inclined to conservatism. Where it has been tried in our country, it has often failed to achieve a sufficiently religious character, but the Dutch Catholics have been highly imaginative and successful in this department of religious art. The Church of St. Augustine in Amsterdam is an example. The exterior is massive and impressive, though perhaps not specifically churchlike, and the interior conveys a note of solemn grandeur that is thoroughly in accord with its spiritual purposes. It is, of course, contemporary only in part. There is a blending with the Gothic tradition. Perhaps this willingness to mingle the traditional with the new is the reason for the success of this experiment.

Maastricht has a very noble example of Romanesque in the Church of St. Servatus. Nijmegen, in its little Valkhof Chapel, carries us back, like Aachen, to the time of Charlemagne. Holland is full of monuments which date from the

Amsterdam, St. Augustine.   *St. Augustine, interior.*

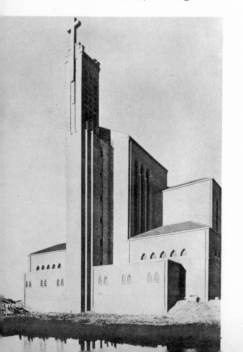

tenth century onward, but its churches of the ninth century, reflecting a time when the glorious medieval culture was only in its infancy, convey to the understanding mind a very inspiring impression.

Perhaps the most magnificent shrine in the Netherlands, and one of the most magnificent in the world, is the great flamboyant cathedral of 'sHertogenbosch. This is Gothic in its richest manner. The church, in large part, dates from the late fifteenth century, when highly decorated style was at its height.

Tiny Luxembourg can hold only a small place in this volume, though in itself it has enough in the way of Catholic shrines to justify at least a small book to itself. The lovely Valley of the Seven Castles contains the Monastery of Mariental. This is not among the most impressive of architectural groupings, but it is beautiful for its setting and is interesting as the home of the White Fathers of Africa, established here by their celebrated founder, Cardinal Lavigerie.

On the German frontier is the famous monastery of Echternach, established in the eighth century, and the basilica with the shrine of St. Willibrord, its founder. Each year on the Tuesday following Pentecost Sunday, the famous Spring Procession takes place. A dancing procession of prayer almost

*alkhof Chapel, Nijme-
n, remains of the pal-
e of Charlemagne.*

*he church of St. Serva-
s, Maastricht, Nether-
nds, dating from the
nth and twelfth cen-
ries.*

*The great Gothic cathedral of Saint John at 'sHertogenbosch. Inside
is the statue of the miraculous Virgin.*

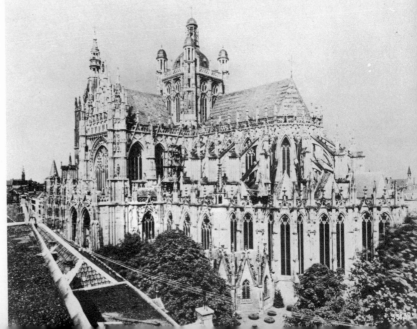

*(Left) Royal wedding in the Cathedral of Notre Da[me],
Luxembourg City. (Below left) The monastery at E[ch]-
ternach, an ancient religious center, restored in 19[..]
after damage in the battle of the Ardennes, 1944.*

*(Opposite left) Mariental, monastery of the Wh[ite]
Fathers in Luxembourg. (Opposite right) The Ben[e]-
dictine monastery of St. Maurice and St. Ma[ur],
Clervaux.*

unique in Christendom, it attracts pilgrims from every corner
of Luxembourg and from far beyond its borders. In the
north of Luxembourg at Clervaux is the Abbey of St. Maurice
and St. Maur, a Benedictine monastery established in 1909
and built after the pattern of the famed Abbey of Cluny.

The city of Luxembourg is dominated by the steeples
and spires of the Cathedral of Our Lady of Luxembourg, the
religious center of the country. The ancient part of the cathedral is an outstanding example of late Renaissance style. On
the fifth Sunday after Easter the Procession of L'Octave takes

place, and more than 10,000 marchers may be seen in the city's flower-festooned streets.

The wealth of church building in Belgium is well illustrated by the parish churches. The one at Aarschott is in a style somehow especially Belgian. More metropolitan is the fine basilica at Hal, and really imposing is the noble tower of Tongres. St. Hubert, near the site of the Battle of the Bulge, is an old abbey church, dedicated to the patron of hunters and a favorite place of pilgrimage. The churches at Pommeroeil and Braine-le-Comte have unusual charms of setting.

In Belgium, again, we can see many picturesque and interesting processions. The ancient penitential confraternities still carry their crosses on certain feasts, and at Ostende the beautiful Blessing of the Sea takes place.

(Left) Rustic parish life in Luxembourg.

(Right) Procession of l'Octave, Luxembourg City.

The church of Pommeroeil, Belgium.

The church of Braine-le-Comt

St. Gudule, the collegiate church in Brussels, is one of the finest of Belgian churches in the Gothic style of the thirteenth century. It is associated with the records of Belgian courage, especially in the World War I, and with the spiritual and patriotic leadership of Cardinal Mercier.

(Below) St. Michael and St. Gudule, Brussels, repository of the ashes of St. Gudule, niece of St. Gertrude.

The Great Market Place in Bruges contains the Belfry, which is probably Belgium's most famous monument, celebrated to Americans on account of Longfellow's poem. Its peal of bells is one of the finest in this land of the carillon.

At Notre Dame de Hal is commemorated the miraculous "Black Virgin."

Not far away is the Place du Bourg with its Chapel of the Precious Blood. This revered relic was brought here by Thierry, Count of Flanders, a hero of the Second Crusade, who had received it from the Patriarch of Jerusalem. Each year on the Monday after May 2 an impressive ceremony includes a procession of the sacred Vial through the town and commemorates the bringing of the relic to Bruges.

(Below left) Blessing the sea, Ostende. The event takes place the Sunday after the feast of Ostende's patron saints, Peter and Paul. (Right) The Church of Our Lady, which has a shrine of St. Remacle, Tongres.

St. Bavon Cathedral in Ghent was built on a tenth-century crypt, and has a tower with four turrets. Its magnificent interior includes many works of art. Its most precious treasure is the "Polyptych of the Lamb" by Hubert and Jan Van Eyck. Beyond the cathedral stands the richly ornamented belfry.

Whether you approach Antwerp by the river or by road, the cathedral spire dominates the city. The Cathedral of Notre Dame, the largest and one of the most important Gothic churches in Belgium, was begun in 1352. It took two full centuries to build the church, the spire alone taking ninety-six years. "The Assumption of the Virgin," one of Rubens's most beautiful canvases, together with his "Elevation" and "Descent from the Cross," are among the cathedral's greatest treasures.

(Above) Orval, a modern Cistercian monastery, rebuilt on the ruins of the old abbey.

(Opposite, left) The belfry of the oldest town hall in
Belgium at Bruges. In the distance, Notre Dame and
the shrine of the Chapel of the Precious Blood.
(Opposite, right) Ghent, row of monuments along
the canal: To the left, St. Bavon; beyond it, the
ornamented belfry.

(Right) Cathedral of Notre Dame, Tournai.

The Cathedral of Notre Dame at Tournai is considered by
many the most beautiful church in Belgium. The oldest part
dates from the twelfth century. In its design the form of a
trefoil cross was superimposed on the original potence cross,
and the Romanesque nave is joined to the great Gothic porch.
The five towers of the cathedral were spared in World
War II from an aerial bombardment that destroyed 12,000
houses. On the Sunday following the Nativity of Our Lady
each year, a procession leaves the cathedral in much the same
manner as the procession in 1090 illustrated in the canvas of
Gallait in the museum. The great tower of the Cathedral of
St. Rombaut in Malines reaches a height of 325 feet. Part of
this Cathedral dates back to the early thirteenth century.

Belgium, too, is continuing its great tradition of monastic
building. The magnificent modern structures of the Cistercian
abbey at Orval is probably one of the most striking groups that
our own time has added to the Catholic world. As such it is
symbolic of the vigorous life of the ancient faith.

(Opposite, left) The spire of Notre Dame dominates the city of Antwerp.
(Right) Cathedral of St. Rombaut, Malines.

179

IRELAND

IN 1932 THE INTERNATIONAL EUCHARISTIC
Congress was held in Dublin. The year
was chosen as the fifteenth centenary of St. Patrick's arrival
as missionary. To Dublin came a mass movement of astound-
ing proportion, the people of Ireland as well as impressive
representation from all those various lands which have been
populated by Irish immigrants, Ireland's spiritual empire.

As one who has participated in this and other pilgrimages,
I can say that I have never seen such intensity of religious feeling demonstrated on any other occasion, except at the audi-
ences with the Holy Father and at visits to the shrine at Lourdes.
The travelers on the steamer, even those who were not of
Irish descent, all seemed to sense at the first sight of land that
they were approaching a place very sacred for its memories
and for the world-wide spiritual influences of which it had
been the source. During the night that was spent rounding
the southern coast and going up the Irish channel, the decks

The Rock of Cashel—St. Patrick's Rock.

181

were full of people, singing hymns and peering across the dark waters to catch any beacon of light from the glimmering harbors that might seem to establish the realization of a cherished dream. To one and all, coming to Ireland was coming to see and live for a while on holy land.

In Ireland we shall not see a continuous tradition of many centuries' production of majestic monuments. Ireland is old in basic civilization. The Celts of the island, like those of the continent, did not have to wait for the Romans to initiate the elements of culture. In the Dark Ages Ireland, as is well known, had lamps that burned brighter than those of other countries. Some fragments of evidence remain in bronze and gold and stone as well as in parchment. But, just at the time when the other countries were struggling into the great productive era of the high Middle Ages, Ireland fell under the gloom of a foreign rule which outlasted those centuries and endured until our own time. This did not prevent her from having saints. Sanctity is the sort of light that flourishes in atmospheres where other lamps grow dim. Nor did it prevent a tradition of fine scholarship. But it did prevent the kind of outgrowth of native gifts in the lines of culture which depend upon the builders' art. Ireland, under the Normans, built a few churches and cathedrals in the Gothic manner but none of major stature.

The Gallarus Oratory in County Kerry is representative of the early Christian times in Ireland. Its size and structure, like that of the towers of the period, are not very suggestive to our modern minds of the use it served. But it does focus things a little better to see a sample of the type of structure St. Patrick must have seen and must have built. In his apostolate, which took him into every part of the island, he is said to have built 365 churches. The number probably would include small chapels like this one. During that period there may have been much open-air worship, but even this required definite places in which attention and devotion might be focused. Such would have been the uses of oratories like this.

Sixteenth-century church ruins on the Hill of Slane, in sight of Tara.

Gallerus Oratory in County Kerry, constructed of un-mortared stone in beehive shape.

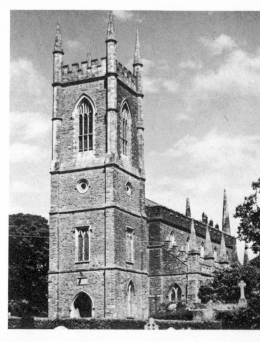

(Left) Ancient round tower and graveyard, St. Patrick's Church, Belfast. (Right) Downpatrick Cathedral, in the churchyard of which is the reputed grave of St. Patrick.

Station Island in Lough Derg, the legendary haunt of evil spirits driven out by St. Patrick.

Later, as opportunity arose and need became greater, larger churches were built. But these, like their contemporaries in the rest of Europe have largely disappeared. This has happened at the Hill of Slane in County Meath. It is told that St. Patrick in his first year kindled the Paschal fire here and that the light miraculously spread over all the land, symbolizing the total conversion of the country to Christianity. A church was built here by the saint. Afterward it expanded into a monastic center of major importance. In the sixteenth century a church was erected of which the ruins are shown here.

In St. Patrick's early days the response to his preaching was such that he was embarrassed for lack of priests trained to instruct the enormous numbers that came to him and his companions. In a very few years, however, he was able to establish centers of professional training. These took the

Large granite slab marked "Patric" in Celtic lettering, said to mark the grave of St. Patrick.

185

(Above) St. Kevin's Church, Glendaloch.

St. Brigid's well, where the saint, according to legend, watered her cows and cooled her butter. The stream, covered over, flows to two oddly shaped stones called "St. Brigid's shoes."

Graveyard surviving from the monastic settlement at Glendaloch.

form of monastic communities, which in his time furnished a numerous ministry and which shortly thereafter grew into large monastic colonies or cities of monks, in which general as well as professional learning began to flourish. Such was the community founded by St. Kevin at Glendaloch in County Wicklow, and that for nuns founded by St. Brigid at Kildare.

The most celebrated, because the most national and non-provincial, of these monasteries was that of Clonmacnois. Just a hundred years after St. Patrick's landing, St. Ciaran founded a monastery and school here which later became the largest and most famous on the island. It was recognized by the kings and helped by them for generations, for these old rulers perceived the value to society of such institutions of religion and learning. There is a beautiful story told of St. Ciaran. On one occasion he went to the islands of Aran to

Chancel arch and nave of the Nuns' Church, Clonmacnois.

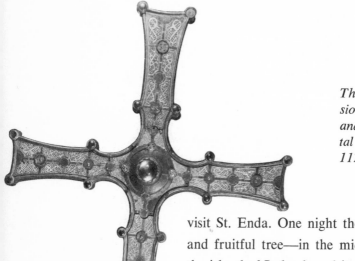

*The Cross of Cong, a 2½-foot proces-
sional cross of oak overlaid with copper
and brass and ornamented with a crystal boss in the center. It was made in
1123 A.D. as a reliquary for a piece of
the True Cross.*

visit St. Enda. One night they both had a vision "of a great
and fruitful tree—in the middle of Ireland, and it protected
the island of Ireland, and its fruit went forth over the sea . . .
and the birds of the world came to carry off somewhat of its
fruit." Enda then told him that he, Ciaran, was that tree and
that all Ireland would be full of his honor.

A Celtic cross in the graveyard at Clonmacnois

The Ardagh Chalice, found by a workman digging potatoes near Ardagh, is of tenth-century workmanship. It is 7 inches high and made of gold, silver, and bronze, inlaid with amber and enamelwork.

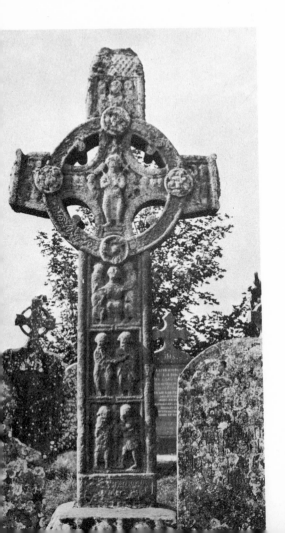

Shrine of St. Patrick's Bell, made in 1091 to contain the iron handbell of the saint. It is brass, decorated with silver-gilt and gold filigree and inset with crystal and enamel.

Pages of the Book of Kells, an illuminated manuscript of the Gospels, believed to date from the eighth century.

Certainly the vision was prophetic. For during the Dark Ages, up to the eleventh century, this place was one of the chief European refuges of religious and secular learning. But it was in the eighth century that Clonmacnois instructed its most famous pupil. Here Alcuin of England came to study and prepare himself for his illustrious career as the chief schoolmaster of Charlemagne's court and one of the renewers of learning for all of Western Europe.

Clonmacnois was more than a school of letters. It was a school of art. Here much of the Celtic gift was nurtured that shows itself in the Cross of Cong, the Chalice of Ardagh, and in the Celtic crosses that still stand among the ruins of this shrine of faith and culture. Its buildings have long disappeared, but the place is remembered and beloved. Here in September the feast of St. Ciaran is celebrated and gratitude is paid by Irish prayers at one of the fountains of our civilization.

From monasteries similar to Clonmacnois came such treasures of ancient art as St. Patrick's Bell, now in the National Museum of Dublin, the Book of Dimma, and the Book of Kells, both in Trinity College.

Among the most exquisite examples of the art of the early

Middle Ages were the illuminated manuscripts, many of which have been preserved and reverently kept in museums and libraries as among the chief cultural treasures of the world. There seems to be a general agreement that the most beautiful of all the relics of this art is the Book of Kells. Indeed, it enjoys the reputation of being the most beautiful book in the world. This copy of the Four Gospels and of other ecclesiastical documents was made in the Columban monastery of Kells in the seventh or eighth century. The original, displayed one page at a time, lies in its case in the Library of Trinity College, Dublin, but recently a splendid facsimile edition of the book was made in Switzerland and copies are to be seen in Washington and elsewhere.

Shrine of The Book of Dimma, a copy of the Gospels.

St. Patrick's Cross, Cashel. When complete, the cross was enclosed in a frame and had on each face a sculptured figure—one of Christ, the other of St. Patrick. It stands 7½ feet high and rests on a base that, according to tradition, was the coronation stone of the Kings of Munster.

Other famous monasteries of this period were Clonard and Bangor, associated respectively with the greatest monastic names of ancient Ireland, St. Columba and St. Columbanus. The older of the two, Columba (521–597), was trained at Clonard, but migrated with followers to the Isle of Iona, off the Scottish coast. Here he founded a monastery which was the chief missionary center for Scotland and northern England in the succeeding generations. The younger, Columbanus (543–615), addressed his apostolate first to the lands of eastern France, now Franche-Comté, where he established several monasteries. His wanderings ended at Bobbio in northern Italy where his foundation again became one of the strongest fortresses of embattled learning in the ages of pre-feudal disorder. His disciples carried on his work in what we now call Switzerland, the canton of St. Gall being named for one of them. For several centuries there were many monasteries in Europe springing from the Celtic inspiration. Gradually they were supplanted by the Benedictine rule which, although austere enough, made more temperate demands upon human nature than the fierce asceticism of Columbanus. But

(right) Nave of the church ruins at the Rock of Cashel.

(below) Interior detail of chapel at the Rock of Cashel.

Ruins of Muckross Abbey, founded in 1448.   *Mount Melleray Church.*
Cloister of Sligo Abbey.

Hoare Abbey, about ½ mile west of the Rock of Cashel, was a daughter house of Mellifont, the first Irish Cistercian foundation.

while they lasted, they did much to implant a strong and positive moral culture upon all the regions in which they worked and taught.

Two famous hills were the center of the early attempts at Irish political and legal unity, Tara and Cashel. Tara was the meeting place where laws were enacted and policies decided that would bring the ancient tribes together. Cashel was the seat of the kings of Munster. It was here that St. Patrick baptized King Aengus and his family. The celebrated Brian Boru was crowned here in 977. In the twelfth century one of the kings, Cormac, was consecrated bishop here. A cathedral was built on the rock in the Gothic period, but there remain today only the ruins and the tomb of the last bishop, Dermod O'Hurley, whom Queen Elizabeth made a martyr in 1581.

195

St. Lawrence's Gate in the city walls of Drogheda.

(Above right) Medical Mission of Mary, Drogheda. (Left) Mother Mary Martin, founder and organizer of the Medical Missionaries of Mary.

(Below left) St. Peter's Church, Drogheda, erected as a memorial of the Blessed Oliver Plunket. (Right) Interior of St. Peter's, where the head of Blessed Oliver Plunket is enshrined.

Maynooth College,
County Kildare.

St. Patrick's Cross is not actually a survival from St. Patrick's time but dates from the eleventh century.

Sligo Abbey and Muckross are monuments which bring us to the thirteenth and fifteenth centuries and to the work of the friars. Sligo, founded in 1252, was held by the Dominicans who continued their work until it was disturbed in Elizabeth's time and finally crushed and destroyed by parliamentary soldiers in the mid-seventeenth century. The cloister is an instance of the kind of magnificence of which Ireland, like her neighbors, might have had much more had history been kinder. Beautifully situated on the shore of Killarney, Muckross Abbey, once a home of the Franciscans, was also taken away in Elizabeth's time, and burned by Cromwell's soldiers in 1652. The friars, however, were not completely discouraged, for they still carry on their work in nearby Killarney.

Hoare Abbey near Cashel was a medieval Cistercian foundation. Here again the ruins indicate how a work was interrupted without dying. For in the beautiful modern Gothic church at Mount Melleray the work of the Trappists (Cistercians) goes on even yet. Here the monks came in 1830, took over 800 acres of wasteland and made them into a prosperous center of dairy farming.

The same note of survival and revival has been struck many times in Ireland. Drogheda, for example, whose grim city walls recall the battles of Cromwell, has built a fine modern church of St. Peter. Here is venerated the head of Oliver Plunket, the sainted Archbishop of Armagh who was put to death at Tyburn in 1681.

Near Drogheda was the first Cistercian foundation in Ireland, Mellifont. It was founded by Irish monks who had

(Left) The Church of Christ the King, Cork, a modern structure with a sculptured figure of Christ by the American artist John Storrs as a portal feature.

Our Lady of Dublin, a life-sized statue of Irish oak carved in a style suggesting Durer. Now in the Carmelite Church, it was partly turned and used as a trough when its original home, St. Mary's Abbey, was suppressed and turned into a stable.

been trained by St. Bernard himself at Clairvaux, Burgundy, thus giving to Ireland in the twelfth century something in return for what Columbanus had brought from Ireland to Burgundy in the sixth. Old Mellifont is a ruin. But four miles away is New Mellifont where the new order replaces the old.

There are a number of places in Ireland today which, though not shrines exactly, do illustrate the forms of activity of the religious spirit in our modern age. The places where the medical missionaries are busy today at Drogheda will someday seem shrinelike as their work takes on the quality that is given by age and continuity. So will Maynooth College which, since the early nineteenth century, has been the central house of preparation for the diocesan clergy of Ireland. So will our Lady of Dublin, our Lady of Knock, and many another place upon which the love of the Irish people has fastened and which will doubtless grow rich and beautiful with the years and with the generosity and admiration of the generations.

Interior of the Franciscan Church, Killarney.   *Interior of the cathedral, Killarney.*

(Below) Cathedral of St. Mary of the Assumption, Killarney. (Right) The chancel, Killarney Cathedral.

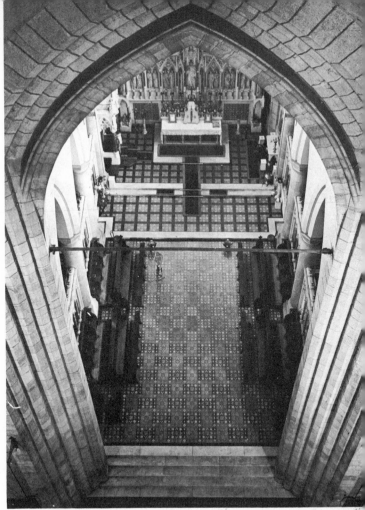

In recent years there have been made some interesting architectural experiments. Only time will tell, for instance, whether such developments as that of the Church of Christ the King in Cork will bear fruit. But Killarney Cathedral, designed by the celebrated Pugin, is one of the few churches built in the nineteenth century in any country which bears comparison for character and dignity with those of the medieval period. The twentieth century does not have to imitate the past but it does have to rival it. And now that Ireland has attained with freedom a large part of the desire of centuries, her people have an opportunity to fill the land with the praise of God in stone as they have long filled their own and other lands with the praise of God in prayer and in high-spirited canticles of generosity and loyalty.

201

ENGLAND

The faith of catholic europe has pro-
duced an abundance of expression, a rich
symphony of beauty of which this volume can only give some
major and minor themes.

The Christian religion reached England in two separate
impulses, the first of which long antedated the coming of the
Anglo-Saxons and belonged with the tendency of the faith to
follow the Roman roads. It is uncertain to what proportion
of the people of Britain Christianity extended, but the great
figure of St. Patrick is a symbol of it. The faith of the original
missions undoubtedly blended with the faith of St. Augustine's
missions to the Anglo-Saxons of the seventh century.

In dealing with England, we have limited ourselves to
shrines which are in Catholic hands or that are still frequented
by Catholics who come to them not merely as tourists but as
pilgrims impelled by devotion. In consequence we are pre-
senting here only the remains and relics of past times. The

The great arch, Walsingham.

Chapel in St. Etheldreda's, London.

magnificent temples with which the faith of the Middle Ages covered the land are still in large part extant, except for the monasteries sacked by Henry VIII and others after him, and except for Coventry, which was the tragic victim of World War II. Perhaps in God's good time the people of England will have the grace to return to the ancient unity and then they will bring back Canterbury with its shrines of Edward the Confessor and of Thomas à Becket, Winchester, Lincoln, York, Durham, and all the rest. Meanwhile Catholics are glad that these shrines of the Middle Ages are carefully and beautifully maintained so that Englishmen can learn from them what the faith of their fathers could create in forms of reverence and beauty.

A few shrines of the old days have come back to Catholic hands and are used in Catholic worship. The first of these is the Church of St. Etheldreda in Ely Place in London. St. Etheldreda was a Saxon princess of the seventh century who married Oswy, King of Northumbria. Her life story is characteristic of those times: a sincere dedication to the highest

Wall detail in crypt of St.
Etheldreda's.

Old altar in the lower church, St. Etheldreda's.

Christian ideals, opposed to the slowness on her husband's part to grow out of the recent paganism of his people; retirement to a monastic solitude on her estate at Ely, where she gave liberally of her means to the upbuilding of the Church in England under the counsel of St. Wilfrid of York. Her shrine at Ely was the occasion for the building of several successive churches and finally of the cathedral which is one of the most splendid in England. Relics of the saint were venerated in London in medieval times and Ely Place, named after the location of her life and burial, was the site of a shrine. After the vicissitudes of the penal centuries, it was returned to Catholic care in 1874.

Glastonbury Abbey brings us back to the poetry of the medieval legends. The story was that Joseph of Arimethea had been sent by Philip the Apostle to preach the faith in Britain, and as always seemed necessary to the creators of these beautiful tales, he brought with him a special memento, the thorns of our Lord's crown. We remember Tennyson's beautiful lines how

Joseph came of old
To Glastonbury where the winter thorn
Blossoms at Christmas, mindful of our Lord.

It seems in fact that this place in Somersetshire was the first center of the faith in the old British (Celtic) part of the island, as distinguished from the Saxon, farther east. A wealth of legend grew up about the place. Here St. Patrick was supposed to have joined the monks and become their abbot. St. David, the patron of Wales, is said to have paid his respects and left here the gift of the Glastonbury Sapphire. King Arthur was said to have been buried on an island here.

(Right) Ruins of Glaston-bury Abbey in Somerset. (Far right) The Abbot's kitchen (1435–1440) with high octagonal stone roof and lantern. It now houses a small collection of Abbey antiquities.

(Left and far left) Gateway and cellarium of Lanercost Priory in Cumberland, founded by Robert de Vaux in 1165. Stone and brick for the building were taken from a nearby Roman wall.

A monastery existed at Glastonbury similar to the ones in Ireland at Clonmacnois and Bangor. Glastonbury was one of the places that the pilgrim Irish monks restored after the Danish invasions. The great St. Dunstan was born here in the eleventh century, and was a monk and later the abbot of the monastery. He renewed the life of the community, and introduced the Benedictine Rule, thus preparing the monastery for its spiritual and temporal prosperity which lasted until the bad days of the sixteenth century. In 1539 its monks were driven out, its property despoiled, its treasures—including the Sapphire of St. David—robbed, and its abbot, Blessed Richard Whiting, put to death in the horrible manner of those days on a tower among the ruins.

In medieval times there was a name which England claimed, Our Lady's Dowry. This title has been revived by modern English Catholics, who think, perhaps a little wistfully, that the assertion of the claim of our Lady will bring back the best things of the past and blend them with the best things of the present. In the old days there was much love for

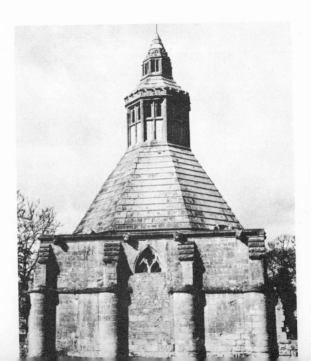

(Left) Part of the ruins of the shrine at Walsingham.

(Right) A medieval holy-water font at Walsingham.

(Far right) The Walsingham priest with a visitor to the ruins.

our Lord's mother in this beautiful land. Many churches and cathedrals were dedicated to her, but she had her principal shrine at Walsingham, erected in the eleventh century. First a little chapel had been built which was supposed to be a replica of the house at Nazareth and which was dedicated to the Annunciation. Then in the way we have seen so often, the shrine drew the attention of many pilgrims. The more the pilgrims came, the more the church was enlarged and beautified. At the time of the loot of the monasteries, it became, like Glastonbury, an object of the royal cupidity. It suffered the same fate, and so did its canons, of whom five were put to death. Here, as at Glastonbury, the pilgrim finds a shrine in ruins. Here too there was not only robbery and destruction of the buildings, but death for the custodians of the place. Here too the modern Catholic comes to reassert the holiness of this 900-year-old shrine.

The Cathedral of the Most Precious Blood at Westminster
is a monument of the revival of the Catholic faith in England.
The faith had survived in broken forms and depleted numbers
during all the penal centuries until the Act of Emancipation
in 1829. With the Oxford movement, the growth of popula-

*Shrine in the Silver Slipper Chapel at Walsingham, built
in the fourteenth century and dedicated to St. Catherine
of Alexandria.*

*American serviceman leaving
the Silver Slipper Chapel.*

tion, the immigration of fervent Catholics from Ireland, the leadership of an admirable hierarchy and priesthood, the building of splendid schools, Catholicism in England began once more to look to the future. That hopefulness was expressed in the erection of this majestic church at the turn of the present century. To pray at this shrine is necessarily to pray for the return to Catholic unity of this remarkable people. It is still, as it has always been, a people of high civic virtue. Much of this tradition it has transmitted to the United States, but both in England and in our own country the social and civic virtues are being tested in this moment of history as at no previous age. It is becoming more evident with every year that the goodness and loyalty of the citizen are flowers which have their roots in religion, and that without their roots they cannot long continue to endure. We have seen the pictures of

(Left) Chalice at the Silver Slipper Chapel, Walsingham.

(Opposite) Our Lady's Brook, which flows by the shrine at Walsingham.

Tower of Westminster Cathedral, erected in 1895–1902.

many shrines, all of which contributed or contribute to the upbuilding of the faith and consequently to the encouragement of the loyalties and decencies of earthly life. Perhaps the pictures will kindle a hope, and from the hope will come a prayer that all nations worshiping at multitudinous altars will do so with one faith, that all the peoples with their varying governments may become obedient to our heavenly King, and that the love of that King, and of His Mother, and of all His saints may impel the future, as it has the past, to clothe the world with the manifold beauty and splendor of new and glorious Catholic shrines.